y**O**1 Exceptional **children**

Monograph Series No. 9
Linking Curriculum to Child and Family Outcomes

**THE DIVISION FOR EARLY CHILDHOOD
OF THE COUNCIL FOR EXCEPTIONAL CHILDREN**

Eva M. Horn, Carla Peterson, and Lisa Fox
Co-Editors

Disclaimer

The opinions and information contained in the articles in this publication are those of the authors of the respective articles and not necessarily those of the co-editors of the *Young Exceptional Children (YEC)* Monograph Series or of the Division for Early Childhood. Accordingly, the Division of Early Childhood assumes no liability or risk that may be incurred as a consequence, directly or indirectly, or the use and application of any of the contents of this publication.

The DEC does not perform due diligence on advertisers, exhibitors, or their products or services, and cannot endorse or guarantee that their offerings are suitable or accurate.

Division for Early Childhood (DEC) Executive Board

ISSN 1096-2506 • ISBN 978-0-9773772-7-5

Printed in the United States of America

Published and Distributed by:

27 Fort Missoula Road, Suite 2
Missoula, MT 59804
(406) 543-0872
FAX (406) 543-0887
www.dec-sped.org

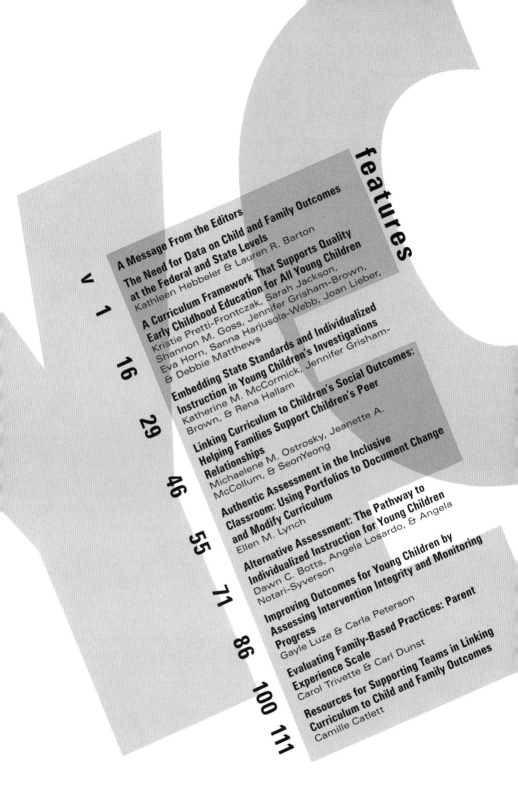

features

A Message From the Editors

Welcome to the ninth issue of the Young Exceptional Children Monograph Series addressing the topic of educational teams linking curriculum to child and family outcomes. Early intervention programs for infants and toddlers and early childhood special education programs for young children with disabilities across the country are developing mechanisms for determining the impact of programs on the children and families served. The outcomes for children and families are used to measure the success of the programs. But how do program administrators, direct service professionals, and families use information gathered on outcomes to improve the learning activities and environments of young children, in short, the curriculum? The content of this monograph is intended to support early educators and others working with infants, toddlers, and young children with special needs in designing and implementing comprehensive curricula that are linked to state outcomes, early learning guidelines, and/or standards. Furthermore, the monograph provides content on the interpretation and use of outcomes data to continually inform and enhance curriculum improvement. As always, each of the articles in this monograph highlights practices found in the *DEC Recommended Practices in Early Intervention/Early Childhood Special Education* (Sandall, Hemmeter, Smith, & McLean, 2005). The articles in this monograph address the values, beliefs, and practices inherent in the recommended practices. They do so by describing specific strategies that will assist practitioners in partnership with families to link assessment, curriculum, progress monitoring, and achievement of child and family outcomes.

The first article by Hebbler and Barton lays a strong foundation for the importance of linking curriculum and child and family outcomes by summarizing some of the critical events leading up to the current federal requirements for reporting outcomes on children from birth to age 3 and their families served through the Individuals With Disabilities Education Act Part C and for children aged 3 through 5 years served through Part B Preschool. The authors then proceed to remind us that although it may be easy to dismiss the outcomes and the associated reporting requirements as a federal activity having little relevance to day-to-day service delivery, an alternative view is more productive. That is, the federal call for outcome data presents an opportunity to put a much-needed focus on outcomes at all levels: federal, state, program, and each individual child and family served.

Continuing the effort to provide foundational information to the reader, the second article by Pretti-Frontczak and her colleagues provides important foundational information on quality early childhood curriculum. Specifically, the authors state that given the continued focus on accountability, it is clear that early childhood programs need to have a quality curriculum framework in place to provide a common focus and understanding of how to achieve excellence in service delivery. An eight-step process is provided by the authors to help guide teams from the initial ideas of the elements of a curriculum framework through more challenging discussions regarding quality, alignment to initiatives, fidelity of implementation, and evaluation over time.

The third article by McCormick, Grisham-Brown, and Hallam continues with the focus on curriculum and linking early learning standards and outcomes assessment as a part of curriculum planning and implementation using a frequently used curricular approach: the project approach. The reader is provided with a step-by-step process for linking his or her state's early learning standards with curriculum planning for individuals and groups of preschool children.

Ostrosky and her colleagues remind us to pause and take the perspective of the other members of our team, in this case, the perspective of the family as we plan curriculum and work to enhance social-emotional developmental outcomes for young children. Social skill development is an important component of an early childhood special education curriculum, yet ways that families can assist in the development of these skills are rarely emphasized. Important child and family outcomes can be realized when children develop the necessary skills to engage in peer interactions and develop sustainable friendships. The authors share ideas about how families can support the development of peer relationships for their young children with special needs.

The final set of four articles shifts our focus slightly to looking more directly at strategies and procedures for conducting meaningful assessment. Stated another way, we shift our focus to the assessment side of the linking curriculum and outcome assessment equation. In her article "Authentic Assessment in the Inclusive Classroom: Using Portfolios to Document Change and Modify Curriculum," Lynch reports that portfolio assessment has emerged as a valuable tool for teachers interested in collecting data that provide a comprehensive view of a child's abilities. Lynch provides teachers with guidelines for implementing this approach to assessment by describing the process of systematically observing and documenting children's behavior and activities, collecting work samples, reflecting on the significance of what has been observed, and completing the assessment cycle by using the data for curricular adaptation and/or demonstrating achievement of specified goals.

Botts and her colleagues also advocate for early educators to consider the use of an alternative assessment framework as they routinely make curricular decisions and adjust instruction for young children. She provides specific strategies for using alternative assessment methods for assessing young children with diverse developmental abilities and provides valuable information for individualizing instruction, monitoring children's progress, and adjusting instruction to meet children's needs.

The final two articles, "Improving Outcomes for Young Children by Assessing Intervention Integrity" and "Monitoring Progress and Evaluating Family-Based Practices: Parenting Experience Scale," again represent a slight shift in focus by guiding the reader to address the improvement of outcomes by assessment of our own, professionals', and programs' effectiveness in providing interventions and services. Specifically, Luze and Peterson describe strategies for assessing intervention integrity and child progress-monitoring components for ensuring the effectiveness of individual interventions, whereas Trivette and Dunst present a tool, the Parent Experience Scale, for evaluating how effectively from a parent prospective we provide family-based practices and support families in achieving desired outcomes.

This ninth monograph ends, as have the previous editions, with Camille Catlett's "Resources Within Reason." Just as with each issue of *Young Exceptional Children,* Camille has provided you with low-cost but high-quality resources for materials to support your effort in linking curriculum to child and family outcomes.

As you read the articles in this monograph, we hope that you are inspired to reflect on your practices with infants, toddlers, and young children with special needs and their families and that families find support for their search for responsive services. A change in our behaviors should lead us toward our goal of families' and professionals' practicing shared responsibility and collaboration toward the achievement of desired child and family outcomes.

Contributing Reviewers
Ann Bingham, University of Nevada–Reno
Patty Blasco, Oregon Health Sciences University
Virginia Buysse, University of North Carolina at Chapel Hill
Cynthia Chambers, East Tennessee State University
Lynette Chandler, University of Northern Illinois
Misty Goosen, University of Kansas
Jennifer Grisham-Brown, University of Kentucky
Sarah Hadden, University of Virginia
Lee Ann Jung, University of Kentucky
Jean Kang, University of Kansas
Gwiok Kim, University of Kansas
Cecile Komara, University of Alabama
Dave Lindeman, University of Kansas
Susan Maude, Iowa State University
Chris Marvin, University of Nebraska–Lincoln
Mary McLean, University of Wisconsin, Milwaukee
Linda Mitchell, Wichita State University, Kansas
Susan Palmer, University of Kansas

Rosa Milgaros Santos, University of Illinois at Urbana-Champaign
Ilene Schwartz, University of Washington

Reference

Sandall, S., Hemmeter, M. L., Smith, B. S., & McLean, M. (2005). *DEC recommended practices: A comprehensive guide*. Longmont, CO: Sopris West.

Co-Editors: Eva Horn   (evahorn@ku.edu)
             Carla Peterson   (carlapet@iastate.edu)
             Lise Fox   (fox@fhmi.usf.edu)

Coming Next!

The topic for the 10th *Young Exceptional Children* Monograph is "Early Intervention for Infants and Toddlers and Their Families: Practices and Outcomes." For more information, check the announcements section of *Young Exceptional Children* (Volume 11, Number 1) or go to **http:/www.dec-sped.org.**

The Need for Data on Child and Family Outcomes at the Federal and State Levels

Kathleen Hebbeler, Ph.D.,
SRI International, Menlo Park, CA

Lauren R. Barton, Ph.D.,
SRI International, Menlo Park, CA

udrey is a speech therapist in early intervention who works with the Serras—Peter, Anna, and their 28-month-old daughter, Melinda, who has delays in several areas. It is likely that neither Audrey, Peter, nor Anna is aware of just how many aspects of the early intervention services are influenced by state and federal laws and regulations. It is also likely that none of them are aware that in 2006, the federal government provided $436.4 million for the provision of early intervention. This was less than the $440.8 million provided in 2005 but far more than the $79 million provided in 1990 (National Early Childhood Technical Assistance Center, 2007).

In the early 1990s, policy makers at many levels of government, including the federal level, began to ask questions about the outcomes being achieved through public investments such as the Part C (Infants and Toddlers With Disabilities) program and the Part B preschool grants program supported through the Individuals With Disabilities Education Act (IDEA). An outcome is defined as a benefit experienced, or what happens, as a result of some action or series of actions. For instance, one can develop statements to express the expected results, or outcomes, for children and families after services are received. For many professionals supporting young children with disabilities and their families, writing individualized outcome statements involves the familiar task of describing the specific ways that they expect or hope that a certain child, such as Melinda, will function after implementing a uniquely designed intervention plan. Then, that child's functioning periodically is examined relative to those expectations, usually when reporting on progress, as required in the child's individualized family service plan (IFSP) or individualized education plan (IEP). In an accountability framework, funders and policy makers want data on outcomes that reflect appropriate expectations for all children who participate in a program. They want periodically to check whether children and families in the program are moving closer to achieving a common set of outcomes as a way to understand whether the program is producing its intended effects. It is this kind of data, reflecting the functioning of all children and families in the Part C and B preschool programs of IDEA that policy makers are increasingly demanding. In an accountability framework, data on the Serra family are combined with information on many other families to paint a global picture of program effectiveness.

Providing data for federal reporting is not a new phenomenon. States have reported data on program operations related to early intervention (EI) and early childhood special education (ECSE) for many years. These data are reported in the Department of Education's Annual Reports to Congress on the Implementation of IDEA and can be viewed at http://www. ed.gov/about/reports/annual/otherplanrpts.html. States have reported, for example, on the number of children served, where services were provided, the number of services provided, and the number of providers. Many states also have collected data on family satisfaction with the services received. Although interesting, these data do not provide any information on how successfully the programs achieved the intended results for children and families. For many years, documentation of program benefits has consisted of anecdotal sharing of individual child and family stories; there was no systematic or ongoing way to report on the outcomes that children and families achieved through EI or ECSE programs.

This article describes events and issues related to the current federal requirements for reporting outcomes on children from birth to age 3 years and their families served through IDEA Part C and for children aged 3 through 5 years served through Part B preschool. The following pages summarize some of the critical events leading up to the current requirements, discuss how efforts to design and implement outcome measurement systems in states presents opportunities at multiple levels, and address implications of outcome measurement for children and families and the programs serving them.

It is easy to dismiss the outcomes and the associated reporting requirements as a federal activity with little relevance to day-to-day service delivery. An alternative view embraced by many states is that the federal call for outcome data presents an opportunity to put a much-needed focus on outcomes at all levels: federal, state, program, and each individual child and family served.

The Age of Accountability and Programs for Young Children With Disabilities

An important event in the evolution of how policy makers think about accountability occurred in 1992 with the publication of a book titled *Reinventing Government* (Osborne & Gaebler, 1992). The authors argued that government should incorporate some effective principles used in business, including the use of result-oriented decision making to fund only those programs and activities that document and deliver desired outcomes. Within a year of the release of this best-selling book, the U.S. Congress passed the Government Performance and Results Act (GPRA; Senate Committee on Governmental Affairs, 1993). GPRA required that each federal agency establish measurable performance indicators for its programs that were aligned with the program's purpose and documented in a strategic plan. Agencies were expected to report the results annually to demonstrate program effectiveness. The requirement for GPRA indicators put the spotlight clearly on program outcomes. For early intervention and early childhood special education, it began a debate that extended for many years over how to—and even whether it was appropriate to—measure outcomes for infants and young children with disabilities.

For many years, documentation of program benefits has consisted of anecdotal sharing of individual child and family stories; there was no systematic or ongoing way to report on the outcomes that children and families achieved through EI or ECSE programs.

The Office of Special Education Programs (OSEP) in the U.S. Department of Education is the federal agency responsible for administering IDEA and for developing GPRA indicators and collecting the relevant data for programs supported under IDEA. The challenges related to reporting outcome data for Part C and Part B preschool were numerous and compelling. Early intervention and early childhood special education programs serve children with many different kinds of delays and disabilities (Hebbeler, Spiker, Mallik, Scarborough, & Simeonsson, 2003; Scarborough, Hebbeler, & Spiker, 2006; Scarborough et al., 2004). How could programs be held accountable for one set of outcomes for all of these children? These programs are designed to address individualized goals for each child; how does one reconcile individualized goals with a common set of outcomes for accountability? How could outcomes be measured? What kind of assessment tool could possibly be used to measure outcomes for the range of children served in these programs? And then, especially for early intervention, isn't this a program designed to help families enhance their child's development? Why would one want to focus only on child outcomes?

The issue of how to collect child outcome data was especially daunting, although many of these challenges also relate to collecting outcome data in the general early childhood community (Meisels, 2006; Shepard, Kagan, & Wurtz, 1998). A vision of 3-year-olds coloring bubbles on a test sheet was not an image that anyone wanted to entertain. Although a variety of assessment tools exist and are used with this population to identify delays, document eligibility for services, and help plan interventions, each assessment tool choice for these purposes can be made based only on the individual child's needs. Identifying an assessment tool that could yield valid results on meaningful outcomes for all children receiving EI or ECSE, regardless of the nature or severity of a child's disability, was problematic.

In 1997, OSEP funded the National Early Intervention Longitudinal Study (NEILS; Hebbeler & Spiker, 2003). NEILS did provide outcome data for several GPRA indicators for Part C of IDEA; however, the study could not address the ongoing need for outcome data. The intent of the GPRA indicators was to see whether programs were demonstrating intended results over time, which required collecting the same outcome data year after year. NEILS followed a single sample of children and families over time; it was not designed to select a new sample each year (Hebbeler & Wagner, 1998). Despite the requirement for outcome-based accountability in GPRA, the challenges of collecting outcome data on Part C and Part B preschool of IDEA could not be successfully addressed, and very little progress was made to set up a system for providing outcome data throughout the 1990s.

The need for outcome data intensified considerably with the initiation of a new review procedure by the federal Office of Management and Budget in 2002 that linked outcome data to the budget process. The process involved an evaluation of government programs with the Program Assessment Rating Tool (PART). The PART "is a diagnostic tool used to assess the performance of Federal programs and to drive improvements in program performance. Once completed, PART reviews help inform budget decisions and identify actions to improve results" (Office of Management and Budget, 2007, p. 1). During the PART process, programs are assessed with standard questions related to program purpose and design; performance measurement, evaluations, and strategic planning; program management; and program results. Scores on these sections are documented next to previous and requested funding levels to support performance-based budgeting.

Both Part C and Part B preschool were among the 152 federal programs examined in the first round of PART reviews undertaken in 2002. Both programs received overall scores that categorized them as "results not demonstrated." (See program ratings at http://www.expectmore.gov.). The PART report for Part C indicated that

the program has met process goals related to the number of children served and where they received services. However, it lacks data on the educational and developmental outcomes of infants and toddlers who participated in this program or the progress made by their families as a result of services provided by the program.

Likewise, for preschool special education, the report found that the Department of Education did not have performance information on preschool children with disabilities served by the program. Difficulties and challenges notwithstanding, the PART review process made it clear that OSEP must collect outcome data for these programs.

This discussion has focused on the need for outcome data at the federal level, but the push for accountability based on outcomes is not unique to the Part C or Part B preschool program of IDEA, and it certainly is not confined to the federal government. State policy makers faced with tight budgets and the need to establish funding priorities were asking (and continue to ask) many of the same questions. What outcomes are being achieved for the amounts of money being invested in these programs? How do we know that public dollars are being invested wisely? Where is the evidence to substantiate the claims that the intended recipients are benefiting from these programs? These kinds of questions also are asked by funders at all levels, including private funders (Harbin, Rous, & McLean, 2005; Hogan, 2001; Morley, Vinson, & Hatry, 2001). Both the Kellogg Foundation and the United Way, for example, have promoted outcome measurement and invested resources in building capacity to collect useful outcome data (Hatry, 1996; W. K. Kellogg Foundation, 1998). Although some may still believe that funders should trust that programs are doing a good job, the era of assuming that programs are effective has been replaced by the era of accountability, in which good programs are expected to be able to demonstrate their achievements. For programs serving young children with disabilities and their families, this means putting systems in place that routinely collect data on outcomes. As discussed later, the availability of this information can serve many purposes, only one of which will be to better position programs to secure future funding from public and private sources.

Building a National System to Measure Outcomes

The PART findings put an end to any debate over whether outcome data should be collected for programs serving young children with disabilities. Without outcome data, the future of the programs was in jeopardy. Unfortunately, since the enactment of GPRA, very little progress had been made with regard to how to collect data on outcomes. In 2003, OSEP funded a national center, the Early Childhood Outcomes (ECO) Center (http://www.the-eco-center.org), to build consensus and provide leadership around outcome measurement for programs serving children with disabilities, from birth through age 5. The Center's first task was to make a recommendation to OSEP on what the outcome statements should be. Specifically, what are the outcomes for children for which Part C and Part B preschool programs of IDEA should be held accountable? What results do we hope to achieve for all children participating in these programs? What are the outcomes for families?

Developing Meaningful Outcome Statements

The ECO Center undertook a process that lasted more than a year to solicit input on child and family outcomes from a wide range of stakeholder groups (Bailey et al., 2006). The ECO Center reviewed existing frameworks for outcome measurement for young children and their families, provided these to groups of stakeholders, and sought input on considerations to guide the development of appropriate outcomes. Stakeholders called for a single, unified set of outcome statements for children with disabilities, birth to age 5. They did not want separate sets for children birth to 3 years of age and for children aged 3 through 5 years or different outcome statements for children with different types of disabilities. Stakeholders also wanted child outcomes to be written as functional rather than as domain-based outcomes. Functional outcomes refer to activities that are meaningful to children in their day-to-day lives; they involve an integration of the child's capabilities to accomplish important tasks. In contrast, domains refer to the specific areas of development found on assessment tools, such as language development or motor development. Finally, stakeholders underscored the importance of identifying global outcome statements because of their greater potential for relevance to the full range of children and families served and also because states would have greater flexibility for linking these outcomes with any existing or forthcoming account-ability systems (e.g., Head Start, state preschool programs, child care initiatives) and/or with state early learning guidelines.

Although some may still believe that funders should trust that programs are doing a good job, the era of assuming that programs are effective has been replaced by the era of accountability, in which good programs are expected to be able to demonstrate their achievements.

Following the collection of stakeholder input, ECO Center staff members drafted and circulated sets of child and family outcome statements to stakeholders. The drafts were revised in an iterative process until near consensus was achieved, at which point the outcomes were posted on the project Website for public comment. Consensus was achieved for the content of three child outcome statements. Consensus on all five family outcome statements was achieved in the EI community. The preschool community consistently supported the first two family outcomes and generally supported the third outcome. There was not consensus among the stakeholders as to whether ECSE programs should be held accountable for the last two family outcomes, although there was consensus that all of the outcomes were important for families. (See Bailey et al., 2006, for details on the ECO Center process and the development of family outcome statements.)

Proposed and Required Child Outcomes

In February 2005, the ECO Center submitted the set of child and family outcomes (see Tables 1 and 2) resulting from the consensus-building process to OSEP for consideration in the national data collection (ECO Center, 2005). The document stressed the important, interdependent relationship between child and family outcomes. It included an overarching goal for children that emerged from the stakeholder process: "to enable young children to be active and successful participants during the early childhood years and in the future in a variety of settings—in their homes with their families, in child care, preschool or school programs, and in the community" (ECO Center, 2005, p. 2). An overarching goal for families also was identified by the stakeholders: "to enable families to provide care for their child and have the resources they need to participate in their own desired family and community activities" (p. 2).

In August 2005, OSEP released what states would be required to report related to child and family outcomes (Tables 1 and 2). Although the wording of the OSEP child outcomes differed from the outcomes that

Table 1:
Child Outcomes: Statements From the Early Childhood Outcomes (ECO) Center Stakeholder Process and Office of Special Education Programs (OSEP) Reporting Requirements

Outcomes from the ECO stakeholder process:
1. Children have positive social relationships.
2. Children acquire and use knowledge and skills.
3. Children take appropriate action to meet their needs.
OSEP annual performance reporting requirements
Percent of infants and toddlers with individualized family service plans (or preschool children with individualized education plans) who demonstrate improved:
1. Positive socio-emotional skills (including social relationships)
2. Acquisition and use of knowledge and skills (including early language/communication (Part C), including early language/communication and early literacy (Part B preschool)
3. Use of appropriate behaviors to meet their needs

emerged from the ECO stakeholder process, these changes did not alter the meaning of any of the three outcomes. OSEP gave states considerable latitude in designing an approach to collecting child outcome data within a given set of parameters. States are to report on the progress made between when each child begins either Part C or Part B preschool services and when he or she exits the program. Data on all three outcomes are required for each child, even if the child has needs in only one area. For more information about reporting requirements, see http://www.fpg.unc.edu/~eco/activities.cfm#Revised_Requirements.

Proposed and Required Family Outcomes

In addition to the proposed child outcome statements, the ECO Center submitted to OSEP a set of family outcome statements that had resulted from discussions with stakeholders. As shown in Table 2, five family outcomes were proposed for Part C, with three of the five proposed for Part B preschool. More detailed information about considerations in the development of the recommended family outcome statements and their meaning is outlined elsewhere (see Bailey et al., 2006).

The OSEP reporting requirements related to families did not incorporate the family outcome statements that emerged from the ECO stakeholder process. Furthermore, the federally required family indicators are not phrased as outcomes. For Part C, states report on whether families indicate that EI services have helped them with a given area, not whether

Table 2:
Family Outcomes: Statements From the Early Childhood Outcomes (ECO) Center Stakeholder Process and Office of Special Education Programs (OSEP) Reporting Requirements

Outcomes from the ECO stakeholder process:
1. Families understand their children's strengths, abilities, and special needs.
2. Families know their rights and advocate effectively for their children.
3. Families help their children develop and learn.
4. Families have support systems.[a]
5. Families are able to gain access to desired services, programs, and activities in their community.[a]
OSEP annual reporting requirement: family indicators, Part C
Percent of families participating in Part C who report that early intervention services have helped the family:
1. Know their rights
2. Effectively communicate their children's needs
3. Help their children develop and learn
OSEP annual reporting requirement: family indicator, Part B
Percent of parents with a child receiving special education services who report that schools facilitated parent involvement as a means of improving services and results for children with disabilities

[a] There was not consensus among the stakeholders from the preschool community as to whether preschool programs should be held accountable for Outcomes 4 and 5.

a given outcome was achieved. This is the difference between a family saying that they were given information about their rights (the help) and a family reporting that they actually understand their rights (the outcome). The Part B family reporting requirement applies to families of all children aged 3 through 21 years receiving special education services and addresses family involvement.

Despite differences between the proposed and required family indicators, many states have recognized the importance of family outcomes and have chosen to collect information on them. To assist states in this effort, the ECO Center developed the Family Outcome Survey, which collects information about the five family outcomes as well as the information required for federal reporting (Bailey, Hebbeler, Olmsted, Raspa, & Bruder, in press).

Using Outcome Data: Benefits at Many Levels

As this is being written in 2007, efforts are under way in states to develop systems for collecting and reporting data on child and family outcomes. Many states are planning to use this information for other important purposes in addition to providing data to the federal government.

State Level

There are many reasons why a state would want good data on child and family outcomes. Programs for young children with disabilities are supported by state funds as well as federal funds, and state policy makers have the same responsibilities to ensure that limited resources are being used effectively. In addition to addressing the need for accountability, state-level data on outcomes can be used to improve programs. States will be able to identify programs or regions that may not be doing as well as other programs and may need extra support to achieve better outcomes for children and families. Data on outcomes can be used to identify an outcome area in which the state as a whole may be weak, for example, in helping children establish more positive social relationships. Data on outcomes can be used to identify subgroups of children or families who might not be doing as well as other groups. The NEILS project, for example, found that all families reported positive outcomes at the end of early intervention, but the outcomes were less positive for families of children with serious health problems and minority families (Bailey et al., 2005). With outcome data available to them, states will have the ability to identify where and for whom programs are the most successful and, conversely, where and for which families programs need to be improved. Because many states plan to use outcome data for their own purposes, they are developing systems that will provide much more information or information at more frequent intervals than the limited information necessary to meet federal requirements.

Local Level

The power of outcome data extends to the local level as well. Local program directors can answer exactly the same questions as the state with outcome data. In what outcome areas is the program doing a good job? Where does it need to improve? For which subgroups of children or families is the program effective, and for which groups does it need to be more effective? What topics should be emphasized in professional development? Does the program need a new curriculum, or does it need to better implement the curriculum it is using? Many EI and ECSE programs are doing outstanding jobs, but some may not be. Even good programs may not be equally good for all the families and children with whom they are working. Information on outcomes is a tool to identify program strengths and weaknesses. The intent of looking at outcome data should not be to punish programs but to engage in an ongoing reflective cycle of program improvement with the goal of achieving the best possible outcomes for all children and families receiving services.

Outcome Data for Individualized Planning

Outcome data originate at the level of the individual child and family with, for example, an assessment of how a child is doing in one or more outcome areas. Whereas state and local levels tend to want less detailed information, the rich information available through a good assessment process is extremely valuable for working with individual children and their families. These data may inform individualized program planning, that is, setting goals and selecting intervention strategies, followed by a review of progress some time later, with possible adjustments to the goals and strategies. The ECO Center is often asked about the relationship between the three OSEP child outcomes and IFSP/IEP outcomes. The intent of IDEA was (and continues to be) that teams write plans individualized to the unique needs and strengths of the child and family. Providers who have been collecting data on the OSEP outcomes, however, report that the child outcomes provide a useful framework for discussing what should be included in the individualized plans. The discussion of how the child is doing in each of the outcome areas can provide an introduction to the development of any individualized outcomes in the general area of Outcome 1, 2, or 3. Similarly, providers have reported using the five family outcomes as a framework for discussing how the program might assist the family in enhancing the child's development.

The intent of looking at outcome data should not be to punish programs but to engage in an ongoing reflective cycle of program improvement with the goal of achieving the best possible outcomes for all children and families receiving services.

Using Outcome Data Effectively

For outcome data to be useful across levels, information collected must accurately reflect functioning, with the appropriate amount of detail accessible at each level of the system in a timely fashion. The distinction between individual data and aggregated data is important for understanding the use of outcome data. Aggregated data refers to data for a group of children; these data have been summarized with a statistic such as a percentage or a mean score. For example, when Audrey, the speech therapist introduced at the beginning of the article, reviews Melinda's assessment results with the Serras, they are looking at individual data. When the program director looks at the percentage of children who have made progress in a given outcome area, the director is looking at aggregated data. In addition to using individual-level data, teachers or therapists might look at aggregated data for all of the children they work with to get an overall sense of how these children are doing as a group.

None of these activities are possible without the systematic collection of high-quality data on outcomes. Although programs have been assessing children for many years, a variety of tools were being used, and data can be aggregated to the classroom, caseload, program, state, or federal level only when the same information is collected on everyone. The new push for outcome data is resulting in states' building systems for collecting, submitting, and reporting outcome data in ways that were never possible before. In some states, these data will be available at multiple levels (with proper safeguards to protect confidentiality and restrict access to only authorized persons) so that families, providers, directors, local administrators, and state administrators can ask questions about outcomes being achieved and act accordingly on what they are learning, given their level of responsibility in the system. This means that a classroom teacher can access data for children in her class, a program director can access data for the children in the program, and a state administrator receives reports with the statewide data aggregated in various ways.

The ECO Center has been tracking how states are planning to collect child outcomes and the kinds of family survey tools that are being used to collect information from families. Information on how states are measuring child and family outcomes can be obtained at http://www.fpg. unc.edu/~eco/whatstates.cfm. All states are required to make the data reported to OSEP publicly available, and nearly all states have Web sites where this information is posted. Finally, a number of states have created Web sites specifically for their work on child and, in some cases, family outcomes (http://www.fpg.unc.edu/~eco/pdfs/Links_to_State_Web_Sites. pdf and http://www.fpg.unc.edu/~eco/pdfs/FO_activities_part-c_12-28-06.pdf).

Next Steps

Despite the many challenges associated with effective and meaningful measurement of outcomes for young children with disabilities and their families, continuing pressure from federal, state, and local sources (including private funders) ensures that the demand for providing ongoing information on child and family outcomes will continue. These demands are consistent with calls within the field for programs to collect and use meaningful, ongoing information about child performance and link it to planning and practice (National Association for the Education of Young Children, 2005; National Association for the Education of Young Children & National Association of Early Childhood Specialists in State Departments of Education, 2003; Sandall, Hemmeter, Smith, & McLean, 2005). These data have the potential to improve policy and practice when outcomes measurement systems are designed and implemented in ways that produce timely, meaningful, high-quality information.

Despite the many challenges associated with effective and meaningful measurement of outcomes for young children with disabilities and their families, continuing pressure from federal, state, and local sources (including private funders) ensures that the demand for providing ongoing information on child and family outcomes will continue.

Building the multiple components required to produce these data is a massive undertaking requiring multiple decisions and investments of time and resources at all levels (ECO Center, 2004). In 2006, states engaged in a flurry of training and other activities as they hastily embarked on communicating state procedures for outcome data collection to local programs. Many states have already made—or are planning to make—investments in new hardware, new assessment tools, or both. New databases are being developed to collect and store the outcome data, incorporate new data with previously collected data, and produce new reports.

Given that many states have just begun to build their outcomes measurement systems, it may be several more years before all the potential data users in a state have access to quality data in an appropriate form.

Much remains to be done in states to support collecting and integrating high-quality child and family outcomes information into practice in ways that are seamless and effective. This article describes some of the key events that have been (and are) creating demand for outcome data. Readers are encouraged to become informed and to provide input to the systems being developed in their states. Events of the next several years will determine whether the potential of outcome data to improve the quality of services and supports for young children with disabilities and families will be realized. Improving outcomes for children and families is a goal worthy of the considerable investment it will take to get there.

Note

The contents of this article were developed under a cooperative agreement (H324L030002) to SRI International from the Office of Special Education Programs, U.S. Department of Education. However, the content does not necessarily represent the policy of the Department of Education, and endorsement by the federal government should not be assumed. You may contact Kathleen Hebbeler by e-mail at kathleen.hebbeler@sri.com.

References

Bailey, D. B., Jr., Bruder, M. B., Hebbeler, K., Carta, J., DeFosset, M., Greenwood, C., et al. (2006). Recommended outcomes for families of young children with disabilities. *Journal of Early Intervention, 28,* 227–251.

Bailey, D. B., Jr., Hebbeler, K., Olmsted, M., Raspa, M., & Bruder, M. B. (in press). Measuring family outcomes: Considerations for large-scale data collection in early intervention. *Infants and Young Children.*

Bailey, D. B., Jr., Hebbeler, K., Spiker, D., Scarborough, A., Mallik, S., & Nelson, L. (2005). Thirty-six month outcomes for families of children who have disabilities and participated in early intervention. *Pediatrics, 116,* 1346–1352.

Early Childhood Outcomes Center. (2004). *Considerations related to developing a system for measuring outcomes for young children with disabilities and their families.* Retrieved July 2, 2007, from http://www.fpg.unc.edu/~eco/pdfs/considerations.pdf

Early Childhood Outcomes Center. (2005). *Family and child outcomes for early intervention and early childhood special education.* Retrieved July 2, 2007, from http://www.fpg.unc.edu/~eco/pdfs/eco_outcomes_4-13-05.pdf

Harbin, G., Rous, B., & McLean, M. (2005). Issues in designing state accountability systems. *Journal of Early Intervention, 27,* 137–164.

Hatry, H. P. (1996). *Measuring program outcomes: A practical approach.* Alexandria, VA: United Way of America.

Hebbeler, K., & Spiker, D. (2003). Initiatives on children with special needs. In J. Brooks-Gunn, A. S. Fuligni, & L. J. Berlin (Eds.), *Early child development in the 21st century: Profiles of current research initiatives.* New York: Teachers College Press.

Hebbeler, K., Spiker, D., Mallik, S., Scarborough, A., & Simeonsson, R. (2003). *Demographic characteristics of children and families entering early intervention.* Menlo Park, CA: SRI International.

Hebbeler, K., & Wagner, M. (1998). *The National Early Intervention Longitudinal Study (NEILS) design overview.* Menlo Park, CA: SRI International.

Hogan, C. (2001). *The power of outcomes: Strategic thinking to improve results for our children, families, and communities.* Retrieved April 10, 2007, from http://www.nga.org/Files/pdf/1999OUTCOMES.pdf

Meisels, S. J. (2006). *Accountability in early childhood: No easy answers* (Occasional Paper No. 6). Chicago: Erikson Institute.

Morley, E., Vinson, E., & Hatry, H. P. (2001). *Outcome measurement in nonprofit organizations: Current recommendations and practices.* Retrieved April 10, 2007, from http://www.independentsector.org/programs/research/outcomes.pdf

National Association for the Education of Young Children. (2005). *Screening and assessment of young English-language learners: Supplement to the NAEYC and NAECS/SDE joint position statement on early childhood curriculum, assessment, and program evaluation.* Washington, DC: Author.

National Association for the Education of Young Children & National Association of Early Childhood Specialists in State Departments of Education. (2003). *Early childhood curriculum, assessment and program evaluation.* Washington, DC: Author.

National Early Childhood Technical Assistance Center. (2007). *Annual appropriations and number of children served under Part C of IDEA, federal fiscal years 1987-2007.* Retrieved March 30, 2007, from http://www.nectac.org/partc/partcdata.asp?text=1

Office of Management and Budget. (2007). *Guide to the Program Assessment Rating Tool (PART).* Washington, DC. Retrieved April 10, 2007, from http://www.whitehouse.gov/omb/part/fy2007/2007_guidance_final.pdf

Osborne, D., & Gaebler, T. (1992). *Reinventing government: How the entrepreneurial spirit is transforming the public sector.* Reading, MA: Addison-Wesley.

Sandall, S., Hemmeter, M. L., Smith, B., & McLean, M. (2005). *DEC recommended practices: A comprehensive guide.* Longmont, CO: Sopris West.

Scarborough, A. A., Hebbeler, K. M., & Spiker, D. (2006). Eligibility characteristics of infants and toddlers entering early intervention in the United States. *Journal of Policy and Practice in Intellectual Disabilities, 3,* 57–64.

Scarborough, A. A., Spiker, D., Mallik, S., Hebbeler, K. M., Bailey, D. B., Jr., & Simeonsson, R. J. (2004). A national look at children and families entering early intervention. *Exceptional Children, 70,* 469–483.

Senate Committee on Governmental Affairs. (1993). *Government Performance and Results Act of 1993 report* (No. 103-58). Retrieved April 10, 2007, from http://www.whitehouse.gov/omb/mgmt-gpra/gprptm.html

Shepard, L., Kagan, S. L., & Wurtz, E. (1998). *Principles and recommendations for early childhood assessments.* Washington, DC: National Education Goals Panel.

W. K. Kellogg Foundation. (1998). *W.K. Kellogg Foundation evaluation handbook.* Battle Creek, MI: Author.

A Curriculum Framework That Supports Quality Early Childhood Education for All Young Children

Kristie Pretti-Frontczak, Ph.D.,
Sarah Jackson, M.Ed.,
Shannon M. Gross, M.Ed.,
Kent State University
Kent, Ohio

Jennifer Grisham-Brown, Ed.D.,
University of Kentucky

Eva Horn, Ph.D.,
University of Kansas

Sanna Harjusola-Webb, Ph.D.,
Kent State University

Joan Lieber, Ph.D.,
University of Maryland

Debbie S. Matthews, M.S.C., CCC-SLP,
Marion County Board of Education,
Jasper, TN

Kamerville Elementary has two inclusive pre-K classrooms in which diverse groups of young children participate 4 half-days each week. The preschool teachers, Jane and Michelle, are asked by their director to provide a brief description of the curriculum they use and demonstrate how it aligns with the state's pre-K standards and how it meets federal requirements for monitoring progress toward three child outcomes identified for early childhood special education. As Jane and Michelle approach the task, they realize that they have very different ideas about their curriculum. Jane thinks it is the weekly lesson plans they develop, and Michelle thinks of it as the published books they use that are filled with activity ideas. Further into their discussion, Jane and Michelle discover additional discrepancies in their interpretations of state standards and federal child outcomes and how to monitor child progress toward those standards, particularly for children with disabilities. Both soon realize that they are not sure what their curriculum is, how to align it to state standards, and whether they have data to show child progress toward federal outcomes. To address the educational needs of all children (i.e., those with and without disabilities) and to meet state and federal mandates related to children's future success, they agree to spend time gaining a better understanding of how to conceptualize a curriculum to serve as the foundation for promoting positive outcomes for all children.

The field of early education is experiencing increased attention to curriculum for young children, specifically in terms of what preschool-age children are taught, how they are taught, and how progress is measured. Such attention is due in part to an increased understanding of the impact of early education coupled with the desire for accountability for funds invested in early education and early intervention (Scott-Little, Kagan, & Frelow, 2003). For these reasons, and the day-to-day challenges illustrated in the opening vignette, efforts have begun to better define and conceptualize early childhood curricula as well as discuss the ways in which quality educational opportunities are being provided to young children and their families (Division for Early Childhood, 2007; National Association for the Education of Young Children & National Association of Early Childhood Specialists in State Departments of Education, 2003).

The curriculum, defined in various ways, is the foundation on which services are systematically designed, implemented, and evaluated (Division for Early Childhood, 2007; Hojnoski & Missall, 2006; Pretti-Frontczak, Jackson, McKeen, & Bricker, in press). Specifically, how educational team members view curriculum affects the type and quality of services provided. For example, if educators view curriculum simply as the theme for the week or a collection of enjoyable activities, they may not pay sufficient attention to assessing children's current strengths and needs or to determining if planned activities result in desired outcomes for children. Furthermore, educators working with young children with disabilities may tend to view the individualized education plan as the curriculum, resulting in too narrow of a focus in terms of what is taught. In general, early childhood educators who operate without a clearly defined and well-conceptualized curriculum do not have the underlying foundation from which to design, implement, and evaluate quality services for young children.

Early childhood educators who operate without a clearly defined and well-conceptualized curriculum do not have the underlying foundation from which to design, implement, and evaluate quality services for young children.

Recommended practice for working with young children and their families defines curriculum as a "complex idea containing multiple components including goals, content, pedagogy, and instructional practices" (Division for Early Childhood, 2007). Building on this definition, we suggest that programs further define curriculum as an underlying support or a means by which information can be classified and organized, leading us to embrace the notion of a curriculum framework. The purpose of this article is to demonstrate to the reader how a curriculum framework can be a dynamic system that serves as the foundation for high-quality early childhood programs for preschool-age children. See the Division of Early Childhood (2007) paper titled Promoting Positive Outcomes for Children With Disabilities: Recommendations for Curriculum, Assessment, and Program Evaluation for a full description of a curriculum framework and illustrations regarding its application to early intervention, preschool-age, and school-age programs.

A curriculum framework serves as a guide for preschool programs in terms of providers' day-to-day interactions with young children as well as a mechanism for systematically gathering data and documenting child progress.

As described here, a curriculum framework serves as a guide for preschool programs in terms of providers' day-to-day interactions with young children as well as a mechanism for systematically gathering data and documenting child progress. A curriculum framework enables program personnel to (1) promote active engagement and learning, (2) individualize and adapt practices for each child based on current data, (3) provide opportunities for children's learning within daily routines, and (4) ensure collaboration and shared responsibilities among families and professionals (Grisham-Brown, Hemmeter, & Pretti-Frontczak, 2005).

Illustration of a Curriculum Framework

We use the analogy of an umbrella to illustrate key elements of a curriculum framework. As depicted in Figure 1, the panels of the umbrella represent the four elements of our recommended curriculum framework: (1) assessment, (2) scope and sequence, (3) activities and instruction, and (4) progress monitoring. The acronym ASAP, meaning "as soon as possible," was borrowed in an effort to support educators in understanding and remembering the elements of our recommended curriculum framework.

Just as the fabric of an umbrella is connected, the panels of the curriculum framework are linked together and create a foundation for all program practices. The functional use of an umbrella is dependent on the panels' being intact and without gaps. So too must a curriculum framework not be missing elements to support the provision of high-quality services to young children and their families by identifying (1) children's current abilities, interests/preferences, and needs as well as family resources, pri-

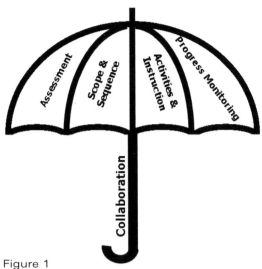

Figure 1
Illustration of a Curriculum Framework Including Four Recommended Elements Supported by Collaborative Partnerships

orities, and concerns (i.e., assessment); (2) appropriate child outcomes for development and learning (i.e., scope and sequence); (3) supports and instructional strategies to ensure growth (i.e., activities and instruction); and (4) procedures for evaluating and tracking children's development and learning (i.e., progress monitoring). The recommended curriculum framework provides a clear guide for decision making, which will improve consistency across the program and improve the possibility that children will achieve intended outcomes.

Furthermore, much in the same way that a metal frame and handle supports an umbrella's panels, so is a curriculum framework supported by collaborative partnerships among team members (Division for Early Childhood, 2007). From initial assessment through implementation of necessary instruction and evaluation of efforts, it is essential that collaborative partnerships are developed and fostered. The process of identifying, implementing, and evaluating a program's curriculum framework is not the responsibility of one individual but must be accomplished by a team. A team should represent the viewpoints of various stakeholders (e.g., family members, teachers/intervention specialists, related service providers, and administrators) and lead to collaborative partnerships that form the needed support for ensuring the curriculum framework is successfully implemented.

Elements of a Curriculum Framework

Assessment

The assessment element of our recommended curriculum framework refers to a process of ongoing observation and documentation of children's performance, their interests and preferences, and family priorities and needs (Bagnato, Neisworth, & Munson, 1997; Grisham-Brown et al., 2005; Neisworth & Bagnato, 2005). Implementation of a curriculum framework begins with establishment of each child's baseline or present level of performance through authentic assessment. The process of determining individual developmental and educational needs provides the early childhood education team with a template for setting child and program goals. At this point in the teaching and learning process, the key task for the educational team is to understand the individual children's current skills and abilities, interests, emerging skills, and priority areas requiring various levels and types of additional support.

From initial assessment through implementation of necessary instruction and evaluation of efforts, it is essential that collaborative partnerships are developed and fostered.

The Division of Early Childhood of the Council for Exceptional Children (Sandall, Hemmeter, Smith, & McLean, 2005) and the National Association of School Psychologists (2005) provide early childhood educators with useful guidelines for conducting assessments appropriate for guiding learning activities and developmental interventions. Both organizations emphasize the importance of multiple sources of information, multiple assessment approaches, and the collection of information in multiple settings and across time to yield a comprehensive understanding of young children's skills and needs (Neisworth & Bagnato, 2005). Furthermore, alternative assessment methods and procedures, including transdisciplinary arena assessment, curriculum-based assessment, and play-based assessment, should be considered (Losardo & Notari-Syverson, 2001).

Assessment of young children's current performance across a variety of settings and situations is needed to (1) help teams prioritize needs, (2) guide instructional efforts, and (3) serve as a foundation from which progress and response to intervention can be documented. Primary examples of assessments that can be used as part of collecting information about young children include checklists (e.g., Developmental Checklist Birth to Five; Early Childhood Detection Center, 2006), curriculum-based assessments (e.g., Hawaii Early Learning Profile; Vort Corporation, 1995), and portfolios or work-sampling systems (e.g., The Work Sampling System; Meisels, Jablon, Marsden, Dichtelmiller, & Dorfman, 1994). Defining and comparing the various types of assessment is beyond the scope of this article; however, recommended assessment practice consistently supports the use of authentic assessment practices and increasingly the use of curriculum-based assessments as the "A" element of a curriculum framework (Pretti-Frontczak et al., in press). Curriculum-based assessments (CBAs), generally speaking, track children's progress toward mastery of targeted concepts and skills. A major focus of CBAs is on the link between instructional planning and providing team members with specific information about individual children's performance (i.e., what a child knows and is able to do and emerging skills) so that instruction can be focused at an appropriate level for children based on their current level of performance and subsequent progress measured over time.

Scope and Sequence

The scope element of our recommended curriculum framework refers to content found across developmental (e.g., motor, communication, social) and subject or content areas (e.g., mathematics, science). Scope can be thought of as the depth of what will be taught. The scope of the curriculum framework is common across children and is comprehensive. This means that all children (those with and without disabilities) are exposed to the same content, which is derived from several sources including developmental milestones and commonly agreed upon standards or outcomes. Developmental milestones can be found in (1) homemade and commercially available checklists (e.g., Developmental Milestones; Centers for Disease Control and Prevention, 2006), (2) resources such as the guidelines for Developmentally Appropriate Practice (DAP) in Early Childhood Programs (Bredekamp & Copple, 1997), and (3) assessments designed for use with young children (e.g., Creative Curriculum Developmental Continuum for Ages 3–5; Trister Dodge, Colker, & Heroman, 2005). Local, agency, state, and federal standards or outcomes also provide a guide for desired scope or content of what is taught to young children. For example, with the reauthorization of several federal laws related to young children, the development of state standards for preschool-age children and federal child outcomes for young children with disabilities has occurred.

Sequence, in scope and sequence, refers to the order in which skills and concepts from across developmental and content areas are taught. Three types of sequences guide the order in which skills and concepts are taught including developmental sequences, pedagogical sequences, and logical sequences. Many skills and concepts acquired during the early childhood years follow a typical or predicable developmental sequence. For example, many children first learn to pull to a stand, then cruise, then walk with support, and then walk unsupported. Educational teams can rely on developmental milestone charts or other resources (e.g., CBAs) that outline known developmental sequences. Early skills and concepts can also be sequenced based on pedagogical evidence or what is known regarding effective instruction. For example, an educator working on early literacy skills with preschool children may provide a variety of learning activities to support an understanding of rhyming, which is recognized as an important part of phonological awareness (National Research Council, 1998). As rhyming skills are strengthened, alliteration is presented, followed by segmenting and blending phonemes, and then, when children are ready, letter-sound correspondence. Lastly, teaching various skills and concepts may at times be guided by a logical sequence. Logical sequences are those that may not necessarily follow developmental expectations or pedagogical suggestions but occur through a process by which team members identify a particular need to address. For example, if a child is exhibiting challenging behaviors such as hitting or biting, it may be necessary to first address the challenging behavior before moving forward with instruction on other concepts and skills.

Activities and Instruction

Although activities and instruction are described separately, they cannot be separated in working with young children and their families and thus represent a single element of a curriculum framework. The activities component of the activities and instruction element of our recommended curriculum framework refers to the context in which important concepts and skills are addressed, guided by children's interest during daily routines (Grisham-Brown et al., 2005; Horn, Lieber, Sandall, Schwartz, & Wolery, 2001; Niebling, Roach, & Rahn-Blakeslee, in press). Examples of daily activities include those that are child directed (e.g., free play or center time), routine (e.g., snack or arrival time), or planned (e.g., circle time or art table; Pretti-Frontczak & Bricker, 2004). Daily activities are designed to integrate concepts and skills from across developmental and content areas. For example, as children build towers with large wooden blocks, they are developing their fine motor skills as they stack the blocks; developing their mathematics skills as they consider spatial relationship, quantities, and configurations of the towers; and communication skills when discussing their creations with peers.

The instruction component of the activities and instruction element refers to practices, actions, and methods used to deliver the content. Quality instruction for young children is grounded in a responsive developmental perspective. A responsive developmental perspective reflects a view of learning in which children create their own knowledge through interactions with the social and physical environment. Quality instruction entails (1) being responsive to the child as his or her needs and personal preferences may change across daily activities (i.e., the intensity of the instruction varies as needs change); (2) understanding the roles of adults, peers, and the environment as influences on children's learning; (3) creating multiple and varied embedded learning opportunities; and (4) tiering instruction to meet the needs of all young children across common outcomes, targeted needs, and individual goals. Instruction encompassing a responsive developmental perspective is dependent on understanding children's current strengths and skills and using the information about children to create meaningful and relevant learning experiences. Acknowledging the importance of development, the varying needs of children, and the environmental context ensures that each child is able to access what is taking place within the learning environment in an individually appropriate way.

Progress Monitoring

The progress monitoring element of our recommended curriculum framework refers to a recursive feedback loop by which changes in children's performance are documented, summarized, and interpreted over time (Grisham-Brown et al., 2005). Information gained from monitoring children's performance is used for different purposes including (1) evaluating the degree to which common outcomes are being met (e.g., whether children are acquiring critical skills and concepts as expected); (2) as the foundation of a decision-making model designed to inform, modify, and revise instruction; and (3) identifying when a child needs additional or more intensive support or instruction.

Progress monitoring efforts produce both formative and summative data that can be used to inform day-to-day practices as well as guide program-level decisions. Formative data are typically gathered on a daily or weekly schedule and are useful for (1) recording children's progress toward individual or common outcomes, (2) monitoring the effects of intervention, and (3) revising instruction. Early childhood educators use a variety of methods to collect daily or weekly data such as writing anecdotal notes, collecting samples of children's work, completing checklists, and readministering curriculum-based measures. Again, although it is beyond the scope of this article to fully define different progress monitoring strategies, curriculum-based measures (CBMs) have been increasingly recommended given their (a) documented reliability in monitoring children's growth toward critical developmental and content skills and concepts and (b) utility in alerting team members when a child may need more or different amounts or types of instruction. An example of using CBMs for progress monitoring is illustrated by the early literacy preschool Individual Growth and Development Indicators (IGDIs) that allow the measurement of early literacy key skills repeatedly over time (e.g., McConnell, Priest, Davis, & McEvoy, 2002).

Summative data are typically gathered on a quarterly or annual schedule and are useful for (1) setting the direction for what to teach individual or groups of children, (2) comparing individual or groups of children's progress toward common outcomes, (3) meeting accountability mandates, and (4) evaluating program effectiveness. Early childhood professionals again use a variety of methods to collect quarterly or annual data such as readministration of CBAs and distribution of surveys or questionnaires to key stakeholders. CBAs are designed to provide a comprehensive description of children's current skills and abilities and can be used to monitor children's progress toward mastery of core content or common outcomes targeted for all children being served in the program.

Identifying, Implementing, and Evaluating Curriculum Frameworks

In addition to providing a description of a curriculum framework with four linked elements, we propose an eight-step iterative process by which team members can identify, implement, and evaluate their program's curriculum framework. See Figure 2 for an illustration of the eight-step process. The recommended steps are designed to engage team members in a process by which they consider the program's curriculum framework elements, ensure its full implementation, and engage in ongoing evaluation activities. Although the process is presented as a series of steps, programs may find that tasks associated with the various steps can be accomplished simultaneously or that revisions to the order of steps may be necessary to best support the efforts of the team.

Step 1 is to ensure an understanding of each of the four elements of a curriculum framework. We have recommended four fundamental and linked elements, including (1) assessment, (2) scope and sequence, (3) activities and instruction, and (4) progress monitoring. After gaining an understanding of the four recommended elements of a curriculum framework, program personnel are ready to form a team (Step 2) of representative stakeholders (e.g., home visitors, service coordinators, classroom teachers, itinerant teachers, family members, community members,

Making the identified curriculum framework visible and usable to all stakeholders leads to clear articulation of the purpose of a program and the quality of services desired and fosters collaborative partnerships to achieve these goals.

Step One: Understand the four recommended elements of a curriculum framework	
Step Two: Form a committee of representative stakeholders	
Step Three: Review the program's strengths, needs, and mission	
Step Four: Ensure identification/selection of all four elements of a curriculum framework	
Step Five: Check the quality of the elements of a curriculum framework	
Step Six: *Make connections to local, state, and federal initiatives/standards*	
Step Seven: *Seek formal adoption and share with all key stakeholders*	
Step Eight: Implement, evaluate, and adjust the framework to match changing needs of the program	

Figure 2
An Eight-Step Process for Identifying, Implementing, and Evaluating an Early Childhood Curriculum Framework

related service personnel, and administrators). The team plays an integral role in the multistep process of planning and establishing a quality curriculum framework. The team is charged with getting to know more about the program (Step 3), specifically getting to know more about (1) the program's mission and what defines their program, (b) the population of children and families served, and (c) the needs and strengths of the program's staff. A primary action or task for the team is to identify whether the program has or needs to augment existing practices to ensure that the four recommended elements of a curriculum framework have been identified (Step 4). Step 4 includes reviewing current program practices as well as commercially available products to determine what is or will be commonly used among team members as the four elements of a program's curriculum framework.

After the team has identified the common practices that serve as elements of the program's curriculum framework, they are ready for Step 5, which is to advocate and ensure state-of-the-art practices and compare their chosen or mandated elements to known quality features. For example, they may need to ensure assessments are nonbiased and culturally relevant and that instructional practices are evidence based, family guided, and developmentally responsive. Next is Step 6, which is designed to help the team make connections between the elements of their curriculum framework and various early childhood mandates and initiatives. For example, as in the opening vignette, educators may be expected to align their curriculum framework to state standards. Following Step 6, it is recommended that the team seek formal adoption of the four elements of the curriculum framework and make the program's curriculum framework available to a wider audience (Step 7). Making the identified curriculum framework visible and usable to all stakeholders leads to clear articulation of the purpose of a program and the quality of services desired and fosters collaborative partnerships to achieve these goals. Last, Step 8 is designed to ensure that all elements of the curriculum framework are implemented with fidelity and that personnel have the necessary and ongoing professional development and support needed to provide effective services to children and families. Although the eight steps for identifying, implementing, and evaluating a program's curriculum framework are presented as a sequence of steps (see Figure 2), the actual implementation process is likely to be more dynamic and iterative based on the strengths, preferences, and individual variations across teams members and settings.

> *Children and families will benefit when an early childhood program has a quality curriculum framework in place to provide a common focus and understanding of how to achieve excellence in service delivery.*

Summary

Jane and Michelle worked closely with their director, children's family members, and related service providers for several months to identify Kamerville's curriculum framework. Defining the program's curriculum using the ASAP model and following the eight-step process helped the group establish a common vision for their work. Initial meetings focused on revisiting their program's mission and reviewing what the program currently had in place. As the group advanced through the eight steps, they continued to revisit previous decisions as they began to better understand the needs of the program. The biggest challenge the team encountered was reviewing all of the available resources for preschool programs. They found countless books and ideas available for generating programming ideas for young children, making it difficult to determine which resources were right for their program. Keeping their program's mission and vision for working with children in mind, however, helped to focus their reviews so that the items selected to define their curriculum framework matched their vision and beliefs about educating young children. Through their collaborative effort, the Kamerville preschool program comprehensively addressed the ASAP elements by adopting a published resource containing the four elements of a curriculum framework and augmenting that with additional resources that allowed them to more effectively address state standards for the outcomes all children are to achieve in their program. In particular, the group determined that the published resource lacked a strong focus in the areas of literacy and mathematics, for which their state had developed early learning content standards. The team found additional resources for math and literacy that were added to their curriculum framework to ensure a comprehensive alignment with their state standards. In the end, both Jane and Michelle felt that their curriculum framework provided them with guidance they need to effectively support the children they serve. The team all agreed that over time, they would need to revisit their curriculum framework to ensure it continued to be a match for their program and community.

Children and families will benefit when an early childhood program has a quality curriculum framework in place to provide a common focus and understanding of how to achieve excellence in service delivery. Regardless of the diversity of the population served, early childhood programs are accountable for demonstrating access, participation, and progress for all children. Consequently, it is imperative that teams broaden their idea of curriculum to include a four-element linked framework that is comprehensive and supports the optimal development of all children. We specifically recommend a well-articulated curriculum framework in which children's current and emerging skills and interests are documented for program planning (i.e., assessment), all important areas of development and learning are addressed (i.e., guided through scope and sequence), and experiences that can accommodate the various needs of all children (i.e., activities and instruction) and procedures for documenting when and why children have achieved targeted outcomes are in place (i.e., progress monitoring). Furthermore, we recognize that differences in how programs conceptualize and define their curriculum frameworks will emerge. An eight-step process was proposed to help guide teams from the initial ideas of the elements of a curriculum framework through more challenging discussions regarding quality, alignment with initiatives, fidelity of implementation, and evaluation over time.

Note

You can reach Kristie Pretti-Frontczak by e-mail at kprettif@kent.edu

References

Bagnato, S. J., Neisworth, J. T., & Munson, S. M. (1997). LINKing assessment and early intervention: An authentic curriculum-based approach. Baltimore: Paul H. Brookes.

Bredekamp, S., & Copple, C. (1997). Developmentally appropriate practices in early childhood programs. Washington, DC: National Association for the Education of Young Children.

Centers for Disease Control and Prevention. (2006) Developmental milestones. Retrieved on August 14, 2007 from http://www.cdc.gov/ncbddd/autism/actearly/.

Early Childhood Detection Center (2006). Developmental checklists birth to five. Retrieved on August 14, 2007 from http://thechp.syr.edu/checklist_download.html.

Division for Early Childhood. (2007). Promoting positive outcomes for children with disabilities: Recommendations for curriculum, assessment, and program evaluation. Missoula, MT: Author.

Grisham-Brown, J. L., Hemmeter, M. L., & Pretti-Frontczak, K. L. (2005). Blended practices for teaching young children in inclusive settings. Baltimore: Paul H. Brookes.

Hojnoski, R. L., & Missall, K. N. (2006). Addressing school readiness: Expanding school psychology to early education. School Psychology Review, 35, 602–614.

Horn, E., Lieber, J., Sandall, S., Schwartz, I., & Wolery, R. (2001). Classroom models of individualized instruction. In S. Odom (Ed.), Widening the circle of inclusion: Including children with disabilities in preschool programs (pp. 46–60). New York: Teachers College Press.

Losardo, A., & Notari-Syverson, A. (2001). Alternative approaches to assessing young children. Baltimore: Paul H. Brookes.

McConnell, S. R., Priest, J. S., Davis, S. D., & McEvoy, M. A. (2002). Best practices in measuring growth and development for preschool children. In A. Thomas & J. Grimes (Eds.), Best practices in school psychology IV (Vol. 2, pp. 1231–1246). Washington, DC: National Association of School Psychologists.

Meisels, S. J., Jablon, J. R., Marsden, D. B., Dichtelmiller, M. L., & Dorfman, A. B. (1994). The Work Sampling System. Ann Arbor, MI: Rebus.

National Association for the Education of Young Children & National Association of Early Childhood Specialists in State Departments of Education. (2003). Early childhood curriculum, assessment, and program evaluation building an effective, accountable system in programs for children birth through age 8. Retrieved June 29, 2007, from http://www.naeyc.org/about/positions/cape.asp

National Association of School Psychologists. (2005). National Association of School Psychologists: Position statement on early childhood assessment. Retrieved March 25, 2007, from http://www.nasponline.org/about_nasp/pospaper_eca.aspx

National Research Council. (1998). Preventing reading difficulties in young children. Washington, DC: Author.

Neisworth, J. T., & Bagnato, S. J. (2005). Recommended practices in assessment. In S. Sandall, M. L. Hemmeter, B. J. Smith, & M. E. McLean (Eds.), DEC recommended practices: A comprehensive guide (pp. 17–27). Longmont, CO: Sopris West.

Niebling, B.C., Roach, A. T., & Rahn-Blakeslee, A. (2008). Best practices in curriculum, instruction, and assessment alignment. In A. Thomas & J. Grimes (Eds.), Best practices in school psychology V. Bethesda, MD: National Association of School Psychologists.

Pretti-Frontczak, K., & Bricker, D. (2004). An activity-based approach to early intervention (3rd ed.). Baltimore: Paul H. Brookes.

Pretti-Frontczak, K., Jackson, S., McKeen, L., & Bricker, D. (in press). Supporting quality curriculum frameworks in early childhood programs. In A. Thomas & J. Grimes (Eds.), Best practices in school psychology V. Bethesda, MD: National Association of School Psychologists.

Sandall, S., Hemmeter, M. L., Smith, B., & McLean, M. (2005). DEC recommended practices: A comprehensive guide. Longmont, CO: Sopris West.

Scott-Little, C., Kagan, S. L., & Frelow, V. S. (2003). Creating the conditions for success with early learning standards: Results from a national study of state-level standards for children's learning prior to kindergarten. Early Childhood Research & Practice, 5(2). Retrieved March 25, 2007, from http://ecrp.uiuc.edu/v5n2/little.html

Trister Dodge, D., Colker, L., & Heroman, C. (2005). The creative curriculum developmental checklist for ages 3–5. Washington, DC: Teaching Strategies.

Vort Corporation. (1995). Hawaii early learning profile. Palo Alto, CA: Author.

Embedding State Standards and Individualized Instruction in Young Children's Investigations

Katherine M. McCormick, Ph.D.,
University of Kentucky

Jennifer Grisham Brown, Ed.D.,
University of Kentucky

Rena Hallam, Ph.D.,
University of Tennessee–Knoxville

In an effort to validate program effectiveness and document child progress in acquiring a set of knowledge, skills, and dispositions, many states have developed child outcome standards that describe a set of shared expectations of what young children should know and be able to do (Neuman & Roskos, 2005). To maximize their effectiveness, standards should make sense to teachers and guide their day-to-day activities (Bodrova, Leong, & Shore, 2004). In short, standards should be linked to assessment, intervention, and everyday activities, routines, and experiences. The purpose of this article is to provide the reader with a strategy for linking a state's early learning standards to individualized preschool curriculum planning with a specific focus on implementation using an integrated project curriculum approach. To begin, we discuss early learning standards and specifically present one state's standards as an example. To provide the reader with a basic foundation, we follow this with a brief description of a project approach to curriculum planning and implementation within a preschool inclusive classroom. With this foundation, the reader is provided with a step-by-step process for early educators as they link early learning standards and plan for individual and groups of preschool children within an integrated project curriculum approach.

Early Learning Standards

Early learning standards provide a tool for states, school districts, agencies, and programs to demonstrate and document the impact of the services they provide and the outcomes for young children resulting from these services. Some state and program standards have been designed in direct response to federal initiatives (e.g., Good Start Grow Smart, National Head Start Reporting System), whereas others have been initiated at a more local level. The National Association for the Education of Young Children (NAEYC) and the National Association of Early Childhood Specialists in State Departments of Education (NAECS/SDE) endorse the use of standards to guide curriculum and experiences for young children (NAEYC & NAECS/SDE, 2003). In addition, evidence from the National Institute for Early Education Research suggests that child outcomes improve when teachers implement practices that are informed by and linked to standards (Bodrova et al., 2004).

In the commonwealth of Kentucky, early learning standards were designed to be universal for all children aged birth to 5 years (Kentucky Department of Education, 2006; see http://education.ky.gov/KDE or www. kidsnow.ky.gov). The standards have been divided into two age groups: birth to 3 years and 3 through 4 years. Each of these age-grouped standards are aligned with the next set of age-grouped standards, so that the birth to 3-year standards that include five developmental domains (creative expression, communication, cognitive, motor, and social-emotional) are aligned with the 3- and 4-year-old standards, which are organized by the content areas of arts and humanities, English/language arts (early literacy), health education (health/mental wellness), mathematics, science, physical education (gross and fine motor skills), and social studies. The 3- and 4-year-old standards are aligned to the entry-level skills for the K-12 (school-aged) standards. In addition to a broad set of standards, teachers and other providers also use a set of benchmarks to provide more specific descriptions of discrete behaviors or knowledge. Benchmarks are smaller behaviors or skill sets that can be demonstrated and measured.

Understanding an Integrated Project Curriculum Approach

Helm and Katz (2001) defined a project approach as a "method of teaching in which an in-depth study of a particular topic is conducted by a child or a group of children" (p. 26). The following five principles can be articulated to assist in understanding the foundation for implementing a project-based curriculum approach: child interest driven, activity based, developmentally appropriate, embedded standards, and curriculum-linked assessment.

Specifically, the first principle indicates that the topic of inquiry must be selected based on the needs and interests of children. Most often, the activities within a project are child initiated; however, teachers may also provide a context for the acquisition of targeted knowledge or behavior if opportunities are not readily available. Child-initiated activities provide opportunities for children to make choices and direct their own behavior (McCormick, Jolivette, & Ridgley, 2003). The second principle is based on an understanding that a project-based approach is also an activity-based approach. Day-to-day investigations are hands on and provide active opportunities to engage with materials (Pretti-Frontczak, & Bricker, 2004). Third, project activities are developmentally appropriate to meet both age and individual learning needs (Bredekamp & Copple, 1997). Fourth, once a topic has been selected and deemed appropriate, interesting, and relevant to children in the classroom, planning should occur that links the project with relevant standards (Gronlund, 2006). It is anticipated that all standards will be addressed during the investigation, which may last from as short as 2 to 4 weeks or as long as a full semester. And fifth, the project approach is supported by the use of a linked assessment/curriculum model (Bagnato, Neisworth, & Munson, 1997).

A project-based curriculum approach can readily facilitate implementation of recommended practices such as providing (1) language-rich environments addressing both print and oral language; (2) first-hand, hands-on experiences that provide opportunities for children to learn and practice skills; (3) tools for children to use for multiple purposes; (4) opportunities for children to talk and write about their experiences; and (5) opportunities for children to engage in work and play that is purposeful and creative (Neuman, Copple, & Bredekamp, 2000). A project approach includes multiple opportunities for children to have meaningful, authentic experiences that provide the context for children to integrate and apply new knowledge and skills. Children engaged in projects use multiple resources, such as print, classroom observations, experiments, and field trips, to find answers to their questions. They write notes, draw, create representational structures, make and test hypotheses, record conclusions, and solve problems. As children increase their knowledge, they test their hypotheses, revise their conclusions, and form new hypotheses for testing. They use multiple skills in writing journals, sketching, or recording observations. Graphs, posters, charts, and other forms of representation document their learning and provide a means to record and share information with each other and audiences of school peers and family members. While engaged in these activities, children also may write creative stories or create representations that are related to the project. Activities are child initiated, providing opportunities for speaking, writing, reading, and listening. In short, a project approach provides multiple opportunities for children to use and apply content skills

Table 1
State Early Childhood Standards in Language Arts and Alignment With Two Curriculum-Based Assessment Tools

	Kentucky Early Childhood Standards (3 and 4)		Creative Curriculum		Assessment, Evaluation, and Programming System (AEPS, 2nd ed.)
Domains	Language arts Mathematics Science Social studies Health education Physical eEducation Arts and humanities	**Domains**	Social and emotional Physical Language Cognitive	**Domains**	Fine motor Gross motor Cognitive Adaptive Social-communication Social
Standards for language arts	1. Demonstrates general skills and strategies of the communication process 2. Demonstrates general skills and strategies of the listening and observing process 3. Demonstrates general skills and strategies of the reading process 4. Demonstrates competence in the beginning skills and strategies of the writing process	**Key experiences**	Listening and speaking Reading and writing	**Strands**	Social-communication (domain) Strand A: social-communicative Interactions Strand B: production of words, phrases, and sentences Fine motor (domain) Strand B: emergent writing Cognitive (domain) Strand H: phonological awareness and emergent reading

Table 1 (*continued*)
State Early Childhood Standards in Language Arts and Alignment With Two Curriculum-Based Assessment Tools

Benchmarks for Standard 4 Demonstrates competence in the beginning skills and strategies of the writing process	Dimensions for language and literacy		Goals for fine motor Strand B emergent writing
4.1: Understands that the purpose of writing is communication 4.2: Produces marks, pictures and symbols that represent print and ideas 4.3: Explores the physical aspects of writing	44. Enjoys and values reading 45. Demonstrates understanding of print concepts 46. Demonstrates knowledge of the alphabet 47. Uses emerging reading skills to make meaning from print 48. Comprehends and interprets meaning from books and other texts 49. Understands the purpose of writing 50. Writes letters and words		Goal 1: Writes using three-finger grasp Goal 2: Prints pseudo-letters Goal 3: Prints first name

and knowledge in literacy, mathematics, science, and social studies as well as to develop interpersonal and intellectual skills such as observation and prediction (Helm & Katz, 2001).

Most important, the project approach is uniquely suited for young children with disabilities and special needs. Helm and Katz (2001) provided five reasons for this. First is the collaborative nature of a project. Multiple roles requiring varying levels of task attention, mobility, and language skills are part of a project investigation. Everyone participates, providing opportunities to make the most of individual strengths as well as chances to promote acquisition and practice for skills and behaviors not yet mastered. Second, because project-based investigations are based on child interest, all children are motivated to participate and engage fully with materials, peers, and the environment.

The project approach is uniquely suited for young children with disabilities and special needs.

This high level of engagement also promotes skill development for young children with disabilities. Third, everyone investigates at his or her own pace and interest; not all children do the same thing at the same time. Projects include many experiences and activities that can be individualized to meet the special needs of young children with disabilities. If necessary, adaptations and modifications can also be used to facilitate full participation. Fourth, because project work is often conducted in small groups, teachers and other team members can make sure that every child meets individualized goals and receives the necessary level of individualized instruction to support independence and success. Fifth, records of children's progress and activities during the project provide authentic opportunities to document acquisition of individualized education plan (IEP) objectives and also document strengths within a context of assessment used for all children.

Everyone investigates at his or her own pace and interest; not all children do the same thing at the same time.

Step-by-Step Process for Linking Standards and Curriculum in a Project-Based Approach

A project approach is well suited to meet state, district, and program standards that teachers must attend to for all young children as well as address the need for individualized instruction for young children with disabilities. In the following section, an eight-step sequence of activities that a teacher and early childhood team can follow as they work toward linking standards with a project-based curriculum is provided. The eight steps are (1) determining the needs of the children, (2) selecting a topic, (3) conducting an assessment of children's knowledge of content, (4) early learning standards-based planning, (5) planning changes to the environment, (6) identifying resources, (7) designing activity plans, and (8) evaluating the project.

Step 1: Determining the Learning Needs of the Children

Prior to any specific planning on the project, teachers must have an understanding of the learning needs of children in the classroom as well the needs of each individual child. This can be accomplished by using a curriculum-based assessment that has been aligned with the state's learning standards. In Kentucky, much work has been done to match the test items on a set of curriculum-based, criterion-referenced tools to the state's early learning standards. This alignment has resulted in the ability of teachers to administer any one of a number of selected criterion-referenced tools to document child progress on the state standards (see Rous, McCormick, Gooden, & Townley, in press).

Recommended practices for assessing young children support the use of assessment tools that are authentic (NAEYC & NAECS/SDE, 2003; Sandall, Hemmeter, Smith, & McLean, 2005), can be used to inform instruction (Bagnato et al., 1997), and are linked to important program and state standards (Grisham-Brown, Hallam, & Brookshire, 2006; Grisham-Brown, Hemmeter, & Pretti-Frontczak, 2005). Curriculum-based assessments have the measurement attributes to meet these recommendations in that they inform instruction (McLean, Wolery, & Bailey, 2004), are considered authentic (Bagnato et al., 1997), and have been aligned with many state standards (Early Childhood Outcomes Center, 2005). The following vignettes illustrate how two preschool teachers use curriculum-based assessments to determine the needs of the children in their classrooms. The teachers chose these tools because the assessments can be administered within the context of the classroom, are consistent with their program philosophy, and are aligned with their state's early learning standards, as depicted in Table 1.

Ms. Christy uses the Assessment, Evaluation, Programming System (AEPS; Bricker, 2002), a curriculum-based assessment for children aged birth to 6 years that includes fine motor, gross motor, cognitive, social communication, social, and adaptive areas of development. At the beginning of the school year, Ms. Christy administered the AEPS to every child in her blended Head Start/prekindergarten classroom. She did so by observing the children in routine activities that offered her the opportunity to observe AEPS items. For example, while the children made sculptures from playdough, she assessed their fine motor skills (opening lid, using rolling pin), cognitive skills (naming colors, shapes, counting), and social communication skills (speaking with peers and adults). When the assessment data were collected for all children, she obtained area scores for each child as well as for all of the children in the classroom as a group. She viewed these data through the online AEPS system, which provides graphs of individual and group performance. These graphs helped her make decisions about instruction. Along with other observations she gathered in the classroom, as well as family input, Ms. Christy made the following decisions based on the assessment outcomes. The AEPS data for Ms. Christy's class confirmed some findings she suspected. Although most of the children in Ms. Christy's class were 4-year-olds, few knew how to write the first letter of their name and many had little alphabet knowledge (behaviors included in the language arts standard demonstrates skills and strategies in the reading process). This was alarming to her, considering that most of these children were going to kindergarten next year. Ms. Christy therefore used the AEPS data to document children's progress in meeting the state's early learning standards in language arts and to guide her planning and implementation of the project in such a way that early literacy was heavily emphasized in every activity, regardless of the content of the project. Similarly, she analyzed the data to identify individualized goals for children in her class and to determine the opportunities for acquisition or practice of skills/behaviors included on IEPs during those project-based activities. One child, also a 4-year-old, had great difficulty attending to any activity for more than 2 minutes. This would be a detriment to his transition and therefore became a focus of individualized instruction and supports within project activities. This example demonstrates how one teacher used recommended assessment practices to guide the development of activities within a project-based approach linked to early learning standards.

Ms. Jennifer uses the Creative Curriculum (Trister-Dodge, Colker, & Heroman, 2003) to assess the children in her preschool classroom. The Creative Curriculum provides opportunities for documenting child progress through the use of 10 goals and 50 objectives for children 3 to 5 years of age. Ms. Jennifer is very interested in her children's use of language, and their progress on the state language arts standard demonstrates general skills and strategies of the communication process. Through interviews with family members and observations of children as they play, she documents a diverse continuum of language acquisition and use within her class. Some children are using simple sentences of three to four words to express their wants and needs, whereas others use even longer sentences (five or more words) for communication purposes. Others use nonverbal gestures or single words to communicate. As she plans project-based activities, she is careful that each activity provides multiple opportunities for language use and expansion. She also plans activities that provide opportunities for using language for multiple purposes (asking questions, making statements, engaging in dialogue).

Assessment results provide these teachers information to target specific standards for all children in the class as well as information for individualizing based on each child's needs.

Step 2: Selecting a Topic

Most projects are the result of an everyday occurrence in the classroom, home, or community that piques the interest of a child or a group of children. The class turtle or a walk by a stream at the back of the playground might spark an interest in hibernation or animals that live in streams or ponds. A nearby construction project may elicit questions about equipment used for building. A child's visit to the veterinarian over the weekend might result in an investigation of veterinarians. Any of these may lead to a rich investigation.

Most projects are the result of an everyday occurrence in the classroom, home, or community that piques the interest of a child or a group of children.

Helm and Katz (2001) provided several considerations for selecting topics. First, for preschoolers, the more concrete the better. Young children need many hands-on experiences. If the investigation is a place (e.g., stream, construction site), young children need to visit often and easily with sketchbooks, paper and pencils, clipboards, cameras, and other objects for recording or observing. Second, projects are typically more successful if the investigation is related to children's lives and is culturally relevant. Projects should be comfortably situated within the typical experiences of the children in the classroom community. Typical thematic approaches are often selected from a list of common topics such as community helpers or dinosaurs. The distinction with the project approach is that the question or topic under study emerges from children's real questions and authentic experiences and the teacher facilitates appropriate, relevant experiences that support the children in gaining an understanding of the topic. Building on

Building on daily experiences engages children in meaningful topics and assists them in answering questions about their world.

daily experiences engages children in meaningful topics and assists them in answering questions about their world. This connectedness is also important in encouraging family and community support for the project. Families can bring in daily materials that may be helpful, and other community members can participate in meaningful and relevant ways.

After children select a general area or topic to investigate, the planning begins. Teachers and other team members consider the connections to previous learning and the relationship of the topic to the lives of the children in the class. For example, in a farming community, children are interested in what goes on in their community. They may select projects that focus on the farming products (e.g., cows, horses, soybeans, etc.) or machines/processes (e.g., tractors, trucks, combines) within their community. As preschoolers conclude their investigation of the production and harvesting of products such as soybeans and corn, they also may begin to ask questions about the use of the machinery for processing and transporting these products. Furthermore, several projects can be investigated simultaneously: Some children may continue their exploration of the farming products, whereas others may begin a new investigation, thereby meeting the needs and interests of children with diverse interests and learning styles.

Step 3: Conducting Assessment of Children's Knowledge of Content

One characteristic of the project approach is the rich knowledge that young children gain from their in-depth investigations—the content of the investigation (Helm & Katz, 2001). Although early childhood special educators typically focus on the acquisition of the dispositions/skills for learning how to learn, what is learned should not be overlooked. The assessment of content occurs at each phase of the project: beginning (planning), implementation, and culminating activity. After the team confirms that the topic the children have selected is feasible, the next step is to determine what children already know about the topic. This can be accomplished through a curriculum web (described later in this article) or the use of a Know, Want to Know, and Learn Chart (KWL; Vukelich, Christie, & Enz, 2002), a visual representation of what children currently know, want to know, and have learned throughout the project. Teachers also gain information about an individual child's knowledge through interviews and discussions with the child. Many teachers find it helpful to display webs or KWL charts in the classroom. Children may independently add new knowledge to the chart or pose new questions. Others use the chart as visual organizations, to review what they've learned or what they we want to do next.

Figure 1
Example Curriculum Web

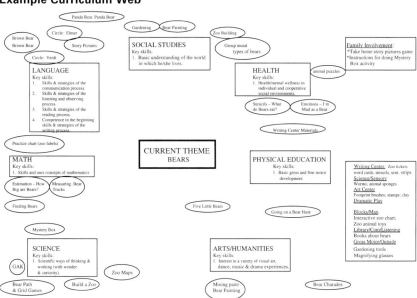

During the investigation, multiple strategies can be used to document the acquisition of content knowledge such as (1) individual portfolios (writing samples); (2) products (individual or group), constructions, or drawings; and (3) observations and anecdotal notes. In Reggio-inspired programs, documentation of project investigations is often reflected in efforts that evidence children's questions, experiences, and ideas about the topic of inquiry (Forman & Fyfe, 1998). Projects typically include culminating activities to demonstrate and celebrate child knowledge through displays, books, journals, and performances for school and community audiences. Thus, assessment occurs for two purposes in this approach: (1) to document child progress in meeting standards (as described in Step 1) and (2) to document acquisition of content knowledge resulting from the investigations.

Step 4: Early Learning Standards-Based Planning

Once the teacher has decided on a topic that (1) will address each child's progress toward the acquisition of the early learning standards (i.e., the desired outcome), as well as the progress of the group of children in the class; (2) is of interest to the children in the class; and (3) has content unknown to the children, it is time to plan. Step 4 involves identifying the early learning standards and activities that relate to the project and allow the teacher to ensure that the early learning standards will be addressed. These tasks are depicted on a curriculum web, a visual planning form that shows the connection between the overall theme/topic, the standards/desired outcomes, and the activities. Figure 1 shows an example of a curriculum web on the topic of zoo animals. The boxes around the theme box relate to the standard (e.g., science, mathematics, literacy, etc.). The teacher who created this web used child assessment information to identify desired outcomes from the state's early learning standards that she can teach through this project. For example, in science, the desired outcomes are predicting, using tools to observe, and making maps/charts. Once the desired results are identified, the children and teacher identify activities that address the desired results and provide a mechanism for the investigation and the acquisition of the standards. For example, in preparation for a trip to the zoo, the teacher and children plan to make maps of the zoo, build a representation of the zoo, and make bears from modeling clay. While these activities will address important science standards, they also address other standards such as literacy and creative arts. Moreover, they are implemented within a context that facilitates children's inquiry about topics of interest to them, in this case, the topic being bears and other zoo animals.

Step 5: Planning Changes to the Environment

Once the desired outcomes and activities have been identified, the next step is to determine what modifications need to be made to the environment to enhance the children's investigations. Here, we refer to both the typical learning centers within the preschool classroom and those activities/environments that are not part of the typical classroom but are necessary to the project investigation. When planning for variations to typical learning centers, teachers must ensure that materials are available that set the occasion for addressing the standards and children's individual learning goals and provide opportunities for project investigations and explorations. For example, if there are a number of children who have writing goals, there needs to be a variety of writing materials in the writing center and each of the other centers that can be used by children with differing developmental needs to record observations. Figure 1

Teachers must ensure that materials are available that set the occasion for addressing the standards and children's individual learning goals and provide opportunities for project investigations and explorations.

shows some of the materials Ms. Robyn plans to use to modify the environment as the children are investigating zoo animals. It is worth noting that the materials address many of the standards identified in her plans. For example, magnifying glasses will allow the children to use tools to observe, and animal word cards in the writing center will allow the children to expand their vocabulary.

Step 6: Identifying Resources

As teachers and other team members begin planning for the project, they also begin to identify the resources they will need to begin the project. Print resources are critical to project investigations. These may include fiction, nonfiction, class or child creative works, as well as informational and commercial materials. Teachers may access print materials from multiple sources including the school, the local community, and even family libraries of the children in the class. Public agencies and businesses are also a rich source of print materials. Other media are also important such as photographs, Internet resources, videos, and audio recordings. Songs, poems, and games are also helpful resources as children begin projects. Materials for dramatic play and building are also critical, as are materials for documenting, writing, recording, and graphing.

Linking to school and community resources is an important aspect in planning project-based investigations. Most often, teachers elicit family involvement through a letter that describes the project that the children and adults of the class wish to pursue and solicits family support and involvement. Families may share their own knowledge and expertise as well as provide materials and other resources. As planning continues and resources are identified, opportunities for community and familial culture and group contributions can be highlighted and integrated within the project. For example, families may share stories about favorite family pets, folk tales about the status of animals within their culture, and information about the care and treatment of animals including those in the zoo. Local community members, such as the humane society, may participate in explaining *Opportunities for community and familial culture and group contributions can be highlighted and integrated within the project.* their role in helping and taking care of animals. Collaborations such as these provide a context for children to recognize and understand the expertise and value of family and community members.

Figure 2
Example Activity Plan

MON	TARGET SKILLS	WORK SAMPLES	TUES	TARGET SKILLS	WORK SAMPLES
ACTIVITY CHOICE: zoo building	J: compromise/discuss S: express opinions/needs	photo anectodals	ACTIVITY	J: compromise/discuss S: express opinions/needs	photo anectodals
ACTIVITY Small group: Modeling clay animals	K: use words/phrases Ch: compare objects	photo of work dictation anecdotal	ACTIVITY choice Mystery box	K: use words/phrases Ch: compare objects	work sample photo anectodal
ACTIVITY Circle: Elmer	B: beginning sounds J: beginning letters	anecdotal	ACTIVITY small group mural	B: beginning sounds J: beginning letters	anecdotal photo

Step 7: Developing Activity Plans

Figure 1 includes the planning web, anticipated modifications to the environment, and potential resources; however, as children explore and investigate the topic; unanticipated activities may be added and others deleted. This part of the planning process applies to all of the children in the program. However, in blended classrooms, the needs of individual children must also be addressed (Grisham-Brown et al., 2005). This individualization component is the purpose of Step 7 of our process.

An activity plan is a modification of an activity schedule, as described by Pretti-Frontczak and Bricker (2005). The activity plan depicts how children's individual goals are being embedded into planned activities associated with the project. The purpose of the activity plans is to ensure that the individual goals of each child in the classroom are addressed while the project is being implemented. Although it is necessary that all children engage in interesting activities and learn content related to a topic in which they are interested, the present accountability climate necessitates that we ensure that children receive more individualized instruction when adequate progress is not achieved independently. Research shows that individualized instruction ensures children's progress toward important child outcomes. When developing activity plans, the teacher may list each child's goals as the plans are developed. Certainly, children with disabilities will have individualized goals/objectives that are part of their IEP; however, we advocate that all children have identified individualized goals based on assessment information gathered in Step 1. For each day of the week, the teacher identifies planned activities. Planned activities are those that are teacher planned and directed such as large- or small-group activities (Pretti-Frontczak & Bricker, 2005). Many of the activities that the teacher identified while webbing will likely be planned activities. From having completed the webbing activity, the teachers are aware of the early learning standards that the activity will address for all children. The individual child activity plan breaks the activity down further so that the teacher can determine which individualized child goals might also be taught. By doing so, the teacher increases the likelihood that opportunities for intentional instruction for a child's learning needs will be addressed. Furthermore, all of the adults in the classroom working with the children are more likely to become aware of the children's goals and when opportunities are available to teach them.

Figure 2 provides an example of an activity plan. For example, on Monday, during a small-group activity (making bears out of modeling clay), one child has a goal to use words and phrases and another has a goal to compare objects. The teacher has placed the child's initial beside the goal so that she knows who has that goal. Often, teachers find that many children in their preschool classroom have similar goals. For example, there are many children who receive special education services who might have a goal similar to use words and phrases. In those circumstances, the teacher puts each child's initials besides the goal. As the teacher is planning, she marks off the children's goals as they are placed on the activity plans. It is unlikely, however, that each child in the classroom will have an individualized goal for every activity. The intensity and frequency with which the identified goals are addressed during planned activities is dependent on the child's rate of acquisition and the importance of the goal. Children who learn skills more quickly may require fewer opportunities for individualized instruction than those with learning difficulties. Children who have important goals that affect their daily lives such as learning to communicate daily needs may need more frequent opportunity to practice these behaviors and perhaps more intentional instruction in the acquisition of those goals than other less important goals.

Step 8: Evaluating the Project

Evaluation of the impact of day-to-day activities and instruction on each child's progress toward the standards, IEP goals, and content knowledge is essential. Teachers and other team members develop strategies to assess each of these (i.e., content knowledge and progress toward standards and IEP goals) in multiple ways (as stated earlier in Steps 1 and 3). However, assessment is only half of the process. Teachers and team members must engage in honest reflection and rigorous evaluation of the effectiveness of day-to-day activities and instruction based on the assessment data. Teachers use multiple strategies during this step. First, they record child performance during the activity as well as collect work samples. If time permits, they can analyze these immediately; however, in most classrooms, analysis occurs at the end of the day. Daily notes and reflections from all team members provide the data for team decisions about the effectiveness of the intervention for the class and for individual children. Some teams meet once a week for this type of comprehensive reflection to ascertain the effectiveness of the investigation for all children as well as for certain children. They discuss ways to support those children who are not particularly motivated by the activities as well as strategies to support the investigations of children who would like to study the topic more deeply or to extend the investigation. Discussion also occurs around the effectiveness of the investigation for child acquisition of the standards and individualized goals. Team members may describe gaps in content areas that were noticed during the week and suggest activities or learning experiences that might be embedded in the continuing investigation and also target learning needs.

Discussion

The use of a project-based approach to facilitate young children's acquisition of state standards and to individualize instruction and intervention for young children with disabilities holds great promise for a number of reasons. The approach is congruent with recommended practice in early childhood and early childhood special education. Teachers and other team members at multiple levels of professional expertise can easily become adept in its use. A project approach facilitates family and community involvement and is respectful of the contribution of families from diverse communities and cultures. It supports universal principles of learning while easily accommodating the attentional, behavioral, language, and cognitive learning needs of children with disabilities. In short, a project approach respects child choice, independence, curiosity, and pleasure in learning and acknowledges the group and individual contribution of every member of the class. Most important, because this approach links assessment and instruction to state and program standards, there is emerging evidence that this process will improve program quality (Hallam, Grisham-Brown, Gao, & Brookshire, in press) and child outcomes (Meisels et al., 2003). In an age of increasing accountability, this linkage is an important consideration in designing and implementing instruction for all young children.

Note
You may reach Katherine McCormick by e-mail at kmcco2@uky.edu.

References
Bagnato, S. J., Neisworth, J. T., & Munson, S. M. (1997). *LINKing assessment and early intervention: An authentic curriculum-based approach.* Baltimore: Brookes.

Bodrova, E., Leong, D., & Shore, R. (2004). Child outcomes standards in pre-K programs: What are standards: what is needed to make them work? New Brunswick, New Jersey: National Institute for Early Education Research.

Bredekamp, S., & Copple, C. (1997). *Developmentally appropriate practice in early childhood programs* (Rev. ed.). Washington, DC: National Association for the Education of Young Children.

Bricker, D. (Series Ed.). (2002). Assessment, evaluation, and programming system for infants and children (2nd ed., Vols. 1–4). Baltimore: Paul H. Brookes.

Early Childhood Outcomes Center. (2005). *Family and child outcomes for early intervention and early childhood special education.* Retrieved May 28, 2007, from http://www.fpg.unc.edu/~eco/pdfs/eco_outcomes_4-13-05.pdf

Forman, G., & Fyfe, B. (1998). Negotiated learned through design, documentation, and discourse. In C. Edwards, L. Gandini, & G. Forman (Eds.), *The hundred languages of children: The Reggio Emilia approach—Advanced reflections* (2nd ed., pp. 239–260). Greenwich, CT: Ablex.

Grisham-Brown, J. L., Hallam, R., & Brookshire, R. (2006). Using authentic assessment to evidence children's progress towards early learning standards. *Early Childhood Education Journal, 34*(1), 47–53.

Grisham Brown, J. L., Hemmeter, M. L., & Pretti-Frontczak, K. L. (2005). *Blended practices for teaching young children in inclusive settings.* Baltimore: Brookes.

Gronlund, G. (2006). *Make early learning standards come alive: Connecting your practice and curriculum to state guidelines.* St. Paul, MN: Redleaf Press.

Hallam, R., Grisham-Brown, J. L., Gao, X., & Brookshire, R. (in press). The effects of outcomes-driven authentic assessment on classroom quality. *Early Childhood Research and Practice.*

Helm, J. H., & Katz, L. (2001). *Young investigators: The project approach in the early years.* New York: Teachers College Press.

Kentucky Department of Education. (2006). *Kentucky early learning standards.* Retrieved June 20, 2007, from http://education.ky.gov/KDE or http://www.kidsnow.ky.gov

McCormick, K., Jolivette, K., & Ridgley, R. (2003). Choice making as an intervention strategy for young children. *Young Exceptional Children, 6,* 3–10.

McLean, M., Wolery, M., & Bailey, D. B. (2004). *Assessing infants and preschoolers with special needs.* Upper Saddle River, NJ: Pearson.

Meisels, S. J., Atkins-Burnett, S., Zue, Y., Bickel, D. D., Son, S., & Nicholson, J. (2003). Creating a system of accountability: The impact of instructional assessment on elementary children's achievement test scores. *Education Policy Analysis Archives, 11*(9), 1–18.

National Association for the Education of Young Children & the National Association of Early Childhood Specialists in State Departments of Education. (2003). *Early childhood curriculum, assessment, and program evaluation: Building an effective, accountable system in programs for children birth through age 8.* Retrieved June 20, 2007, from http://www.naeyc.org/resources/position_statements/CAPEexpand.pdf

Neuman, S., Copple, C., & Bredekamp, S. (2000). *Learning to read and write: Developmentally appropriate practices for young children.* Washington, DC: National Association for the Education of Young Children.

Neuman, S. B., & Roskos, K. (2005). The state of state pre-kindergarten standards. *Early Childhood Research Quarterly, (20)*2, 125–145.

Pretti-Frontczak, K., & Bricker, D. (2004). *An activity-based approach to early intervention* (3rd ed.). Baltimore: Brookes.

Rous, B., McCormick, K., Gooden, C., & Townley, K. (2007). Kentucky's early childhood continuous assessment system: Local decisions and state supports. *Topics in Early Childhood Special Education, 27*(1), 19–33.

Sandall, S., Hemmeter, M. L., Smith, B. J., & McLean, M. (2005). *DEC recommended practices: A comprehensive guide.* Longmont, CO: Sopris West.

Trister-Dodge, D., Colker, L., & Heroman, C. (2003). *The Creative Curriculum for preschool,* (4th ed.). Washington, DC: Teaching Strategies Inc.

Vukelich, C., Christie, J., & Enz, B. (2002). *Helping young children learn language and literacy.* Boston: Allyn & Bacon.

Linking Curriculum to Children's Social Outcomes: Helping Families Support Children's Peer Relationships

Michaelene M. Ostrosky, Ph.D.,

Jeanette A. McCollum, Ph.D.,

SeonYeong Yu, M.S.,
University of Illinois, Urbana-Champaign

Kendall, a red-headed, happy-go-lucky first grader, is the only child of Mike and Jacki. Kendall has multiple disabilities that significantly affect her communication and social skills. She rarely gets invited by her classmates for play dates, birthday parties, or other special activities. Although Mike and Jacki frequently take Kendall to the park near their house, she seldom interacts with other children while there. Instead, Kendall will watch the other children from afar, occasionally grabbing a sandbox toy and running from the children with it. Mike and Jacki find themselves constantly wondering what they can do to support their young daughter's development of friendships.

A variety of skills contribute to young children's social-emotional competence (Halberstadt, Denham, & Dunsmore, 2001; Hubbard & Coie, 1994). For example, the ability to persist at tasks and follow directions has been identified as an important component of social-emotional competence. In addition, the capacity to identify, understand, and communicate feelings and the ability to constructively manage emotions and to be empathetic are critical skills. Finally, the ability to develop positive relationships with peers and adults is described as an important social-emotional skill.

Establishing friendships in early childhood is a major developmental task and predicts later adjustment (Danko & Buysee, 2002). Early childhood teachers have a responsibility to provide environments that support friendship development. For example, one of the child-focused recommended practices identified by the Division for Early Childhood (DEC) of the Council for Exceptional Children (Sandall, Hemmeter, Smith, & McLean, 2005) is "environments are provided that foster positive relationships, including peer-peer, parents/caregivers-child, and parent-caregiver relationships" (p. 83). Likewise, the National Association for the Education of Young Children (NAEYC) guidelines state that "developmentally appropriate practices support the development of relationships between adults and children, among children, among teachers, and between families and teachers" (Bredekamp & Copple, 1987). Clearly, the leading early childhood special education (i.e., DEC) and early childhood (i.e., NAEYC) international organizations view peer relationships as hallmarks of early childhood development.

During the early years, children's friendships have significant implications for cognitive, communicative, and social development as well as for an emerging sense of self (Guralnick, Connor, & Hammond, 1995). Friendships benefit children by facilitating learning, enhancing a sense of belonging, and lessening stress (Overton & Rausch, 2002). In addition, successful friendships and peer relationships in early childhood influence children's quality of life (Meyer, Park, Grenot-Scheyer, Schwartz, & Harry, 1998).

Many children with disabilities experience difficulties engaging in social interactions and developing relationships with their peers. Interest in the friendships of children with disabilities has increased along with the inclusive education movement (Taylor, Peterson, McMurray-Schwarz, & Guillou, 2002). In addition, researchers have suggested ways to improve social interactions and facilitate relationships between children with and without disabilities (e.g., Kohler, Anthony, Steighner, & Hoyson, 2001).

Although much of the research regarding the friendships of children with disabilities focuses on school settings (Geisthardt, Brotherson, & Cook, 2002), research and practice in special education are evolving to include a focus on the development of friendships that extend beyond the basic social interactions that typically occur in inclusive settings (Richardson & Schwart, 1998). Children with disabilities have opportunities to interact with their peers and make friends near their homes and in their communities. Parents of children with disabilities have stated that having their children learn to interact socially with peers and develop friendships is an important priority (Guralnick et al., 1995). However, there is little research focusing on parents' facilitation of friendships for young children with disabilities. Turnbull, Pereira, and Blue-Banning (1999) noted that even though children with disabilities have a great need for friendship development, there has been virtually no research on parents' support of such friendships.

Research on parents' perspectives about the friendships of their children with disabilities mainly describes how important parents perceive these friendships to be (Overton & Rausch, 2002), the factors that parents report influence friendship formation (Guralnick et al., 1995), and friendship characteristics described by parents (Staub, Schwartz, Gallucci, & Peck, 1994). Strully and Strully (1996) stated that parents believe friendships are possible and critical for children's quality of life. Yet many parents believe that limited social skills can obstruct friendship formation (Strully & Strully, 1996; Turnbull et al., 1999).

Parents believe friendships are possible and critical for children's quality of life.

The results from several research studies indicate that parents of typically developing children can affect friendships between children with and without disabilities, especially when children are young (Geisthardt et al., 2002; Staub et al., 1994). Geisthardt and colleagues (2002) found that the attitudes of parents toward the importance of facilitating friendships were very important to friendship development in typically developing children. In addition, Staub and colleagues (1994) noted that parents of typically developing children often assumed supportive roles for friendship development between children with and without disabilities.

The purpose of this article is to share ideas about how families can support the development of peer relationships for their young children with special needs. Social skill development is an important component of an early childhood special education curriculum, yet the ways that families can assist in the development of these skills is rarely emphasized. Important child and family outcomes can be realized when children develop the necessary skills to engage in peer interactions and develop sustainable friendships. In reviewing the research, it is evident that family members directly and indirectly influence their children's peer relations in three important ways: (1) through parent-child interactions; (2) through taking roles as supervisors, coaches, and advisers; and (3) through taking roles as providers of social opportunities (McCollum & Ostrosky, in press). Table 1 provides some more detail across these three pathways of influence. In the following sections, ideas for how parents can support the peer relationships of their children across each of these three pathways of influence are presented. Early childhood educators might consider sharing these ideas with interested families whose children need additional support in developing positive relationships with peers. Individual child and family characteristics should always be taken into account when designing curriculum, including curriculum across school-home contexts, to support social outcomes.

Table 1
Three Pathways of Influence: Parents Supporting Peer Relationships

Pathway	Examples
Through parent-child interactions	• Using strategies that facilitate emotional regulation (e.g., discussing "how would you feel if . . . ," "what makes you feel proud/angry/frustrated/excited, etc.," and "what would you do if . . .," reading books that discuss emotions) • Participating in activities that support parent-child interactions such as engaging in turn-taking and establishing joint attention
Through parents' roles as supervisors, coaches, and advisers	• Helping with the flow of interactions, maintaining a child's interest in play, prompting specific social behaviors, preventing conflict • Organizing play activities • Including siblings, siblings' friends, and cousins in interactions
Through parents' roles as providers of social opportunities	• Organizing or participating in social opportunities such as play dates, birthday parties, community-based activities (e.g., library activities, swimming classes, neighborhood playgrounds, science clubs, Girl Scouts, sports activities, chess club, faith-based activities, potlucks)

Supporting Peer Relationships Through Parent-Child Interactions

The child development literature provides an important context for understanding parent-child and child-peer relationships. Parents affect the friendship development of their young children in many ways (Geisthardt et al., 2002). For example, positive parent-child relationships predict peer acceptance and popularity, whereas nonsupportive parent-child relationships are related to peer rejection and aggressive behavior (Clark & Ladd, 2000; Youngblade & Belsky, 1992). Research on typically developing children and their parents shows that parenting style (through everyday parent-child interactions) influences children's ability to understand and interpret affective cues, regulate their own emotions, and learn appropriate interaction skills (Parke, Burks, Carson, Neville, & Boyum, 1994). Any or all of these skills may contribute to children's competence with peers. Although the research is limited on parents of children with special needs, there is reason to believe that these important parent-child relationships have the potential to affect peer acceptance and social relationships. Thus, early educators can provide families with tips and information on how, through their own interactions with their children, they can support their children's development of important skills that will contribute to their competence as they interact with peers.

In returning to our opening vignette, we can see how Kendall's family, with support from their early education team, works on social competence skills through their own interactions with Kendall (e.g., turn-taking, establishing joint attention to toys). Jacki and Mike continuously work with Kendall on regulating her emotions and interpreting the emotions of others. For example, Mike and Jacki talk with Kendall about a range of feelings that extend beyond happy, mad, and sad, and they read children's books that discuss emotions (e.g., Glad Monster Sad Monster, On Monday When It Rains) that the early childhood educator has recommended to them. In addition, they anticipate situations that might be stressful for Kendall and are available to help her problem solve and use her words. Mike and Jacki also work with Kendall to read their facial cues to help her understand that nonverbal cues are important insights into how people feel.

Supporting Peer Relationships as Supervisors, Coaches, and Advisers

Parents can intentionally, directly, and explicitly influence their children's peer interactions by supervising and advising their children's interactions. For example, a parent may participate in peer play as a play partner, helping the flow of the interaction by establishing turn taking, maintaining a child's interest in a peer or in play, prompting specific behaviors, and/or preventing conflicts or disruptions (Lollis, Ross, & Tate, 1992). Bhavnagri and Parke (1985, 1991) found that younger children benefited more from parent intervention strategies related to initiating and turn taking and that older children benefited more from assistance with maintaining play.

Parents also influence their children's peer interactions using indirect strategies such as monitoring (Lawhon & Lawhon, 2000). Parents can act as observers rather than active participants during peer play interactions. For example, as parents supervise their children's play, they might offer subtle ideas for organizing the play activities (e.g., "Kendall and Maggie, why don't the two of you build a zoo for the plastic animals with the blocks? Maggie, you build some cages for the monkeys, and Kendall, you build an area for the bears."). Young children's social competence and play interactions can be enhanced through parents' interactive and directive monitoring.

In addition to participating in or supervising peer play, parents also may serve as advisers or consultants through conversations about peer interactions that occur outside of that context (Lollis et al., 1992). For example, parents may engage children in conversations about how to manage conflicts or may help children think about how they could have resolved previous conflicts (e.g., "Kendall, let's think about ways you can ask Aubrey for a turn the next time she has something you want to play with.").

Geisthardt et al. (2002) indicated that mothers' supervision of peer interactions were primarily indirect, with intervention occurring mainly when there was a disagreement. However, given the social skills difficulties that many children with disabilities have, indirect supervision may not be the most effective way for parents to support their children's peer interactions. It may be that parents who assume more interactive roles in their children's play enable children to enact and learn higher level play skills and social skills.

Again, as we return to the opening vignette, we can see how Kendall's parents have created opportunities for Kendall to play with peers and extend and practice the skills that she is learning in her preschool setting.

When Mike and Jacki invite neighborhood children over to play, they supervise and facilitate Kendall's social interactions with these children. Together with the early educator, they have identified strategies through ongoing monitoring that they can use to prevent problems from arising. If problems arise, they are available to address conflicts and help generate solutions that result in positive outcomes.

Supporting Peer Relationships as Providers of Social Opportunities

Although siblings and relatives (e.g., cousins) can provide a natural context for the development of peer interaction skills, children also gain important benefits from interacting with children outside of the family (Ladd & Pettit, 2002). Parents can directly or indirectly provide their children with social opportunities that set the foundation for peer interaction. For example, parents can arrange opportunities for interactions with typically developing peers by organizing play dates and playgroups. By setting up activities that are enticing and fun, parents are likely to create an environ-

Parents can directly or indirectly provide their children with social opportunities that set the foundation for peer interaction.

ment that draws peers to it, as in the example from Kendall's family that follows.

Mike, a talented artist, has been teaching Kendall to paint and work with clay. He and Jacki frequently invite neighborhood children over to do art activities. By structuring the art projects and limiting the materials (e.g., limited number of paintbrushes so children share, one easel so children paint together), Mike and Jacki encourage Kendall to interact with children her age, and they facilitate the development of numerous social skills (e.g., turn taking, sharing, asking for assistance, maintaining interactions, initiating).

The early education team can also help families to take advantage of community activities. For example, families of young children with special needs might take their children to library activities, free concerts, and neighborhood playgrounds. Also, by providing families with information about available extracurricular and community-based activities that are often structured according to age or skill level (e.g., science club, Girl Scouts, sports activities, chess club, faith-based activities, camps), early educators can help families find additional opportunities to expose their children to a variety of potential friends. Potlucks with friends who have young children provide another venue for potential playmates, and as children observe adults interacting with each other, children can see social skills naturally being modeled for them. In addition, the friends of siblings can provide opportunities that support the development of social competence.

Advocating for and ensuring that young children with disabilities are included and attend programs and schools in their neighborhoods alongside their neighborhood peers are important components for supporting the development of friendships. Neighborhood schools provide opportunities for children to develop relationships with age mates who live within close proximity, thereby increasing the possibility of peer interactions.

Conclusion

Although curriculum typically is defined as the content areas of instruction for children (e.g., social skills, motor skills) and the teaching practices or methods used by adults within school settings (e.g., modeling, nonverbal prompting), there is no reason to limit the instructional context to educational settings. Parents and other caregivers can support the development of

Parents and other caregivers can support the development of peer relationships, an important outcome of adequate social skills, in a variety of ways.

peer relationships, an important outcome of adequate social skills, in a variety of ways as described above. Teachers can influence the development of peer-related prosocial skills by sharing ideas with interested family members.

The three pathways of parent influence presented in this article offer a novel perspective on supporting children's peer interactions by highlighting developmental origins of social competence within family relationships (McCollum & Ostrosky, in press). These pathways provide guidance for intervention, promotion, and prevention while taking into account contextual variables such as family characteristics (e.g., parental education, financial resources, social supports, culture) and family patterns of interaction (Guralnick, 2005). From children's earliest ages, parents can be assisted in taking advantage of potential opportunities for peer interaction within their own family, friendship groups, neighborhood networks, and the community. Additional social opportunities may need to be created through formats such as playgroups and play dates. Interventions that support families who value peer relationships may influence young children's peer-related social competence.

Note

The preparation of this article was supported by the Center on the Social and Emotional Foundations for Early Learning, U.S. Department of Health and Human Services (PHS SubVU19247). You can reach Michaelene M. Ostrosky by e-mail at ostrosky@uiuc.edu.

References

Bhavnagri, N., & Parke, R. D. (1985). *Parents as facilitators of preschool peer interaction.* Paper presented at the Biennial Meeting of the Society for Research in Child Development, Toronto, Canada.

Bhavnagri, N., & Parke, R. D. (1991). Parents as direct facilitators of children's peer relationships: Effects of age of child and sex of parent. *Journal of Social and Personal Relationships, 8,* 423–440.

Bredekamp, S., & Copple, C. (Eds.). (1997). *Developmentally appropriate practices in early childhood programs* (Rev. ed.). Washington, DC: National Association for the Education of Young Children.

Clark, K. E., & Ladd, G. W. (2000). Connectedness and autonomy support in parent-child relationships: Links to children's socioemotional orientation and peer relationships. *Developmental Psychology, 36,* 485–498.

Danko, C. D., & Buysse, V. (2002). Thank you for being a friend. *Young Exceptional Children, 6,* 2–9.

Geisthardt, C. L., Brotherson, M. J., & Cook, C. C. (2002). Friendships of children with disabilities in the home environment. *Education and Training in Mental Retardation and Developmental Disabilities, 37,* 235–252.

Guralnick, M. J. (2005). Early intervention for children with intellectual disabilities: Current knowledge and future prospects. *Journal of Applied Research in Intellectual Disabilities, 18,* 313–324.

Guralnick, M. J., Connor, R. T., & Hammond, M. (1995). Parent perspectives of peer relationships and friendships in integrated and specialized programs. *American Journal on Mental Retardation, 99,* 457–476.

Halberstadt, A. G., Denham, S. A., & Dunsmore, J. C. (2001). Affective social competence. *Social Development, 10,* 79–119.

Hubbard, J. A., & Coie, J. D. (1994). Emotional correlates of social competence in children's peer relationships. *Merrill-Palmer Quarterly, 50,* 1–20.

Kohler, F. W., Anthony, L. J., Steighner, S. A., & Hoyson, M. (2001). Teaching social interaction skills in the integrated preschool: An examination of naturalistic tactics. *Topics in Early Childhood Special Education, 21,* 93–103.

Ladd, G. W., & Pettit, G. S. (2002). Parenting and the development of children's peer relationships. In M. Bornstein (Ed.), *Handbook of parenting, volume 5: Practical issues in parenting* (pp. 269–309). Mahway, NJ: Lawrence Erlbaum Associates.

Lawhon, T., & Lawhon, D. C. (2000). Promoting social skills in young children. *Early Childhood Education Journal, 28,* 105–117.

Lollis, S. P., Ross, H. S., & Tate, E. (1992). Parents' regulation of children's peer interactions: Direct influences. In R. D. Parke & G. W. Ladd (Eds.), *Family-peer relationships: Modes of linkage* (pp. 255–281). Mahway, NJ: Lawrence Erlbaum Associates.

McCollum, J. A., & Ostrosky, M. M. (in press). Family roles in young children's emerging peer-related social competence. In W. Brown, S. R. McConnell, & S. L. Odom (Eds.), *Peer-related social competence*. Baltimore: Brookes.

Meyer, L. H., Park, H., Grenot-Scheyer, M., Schwartz, I. S., & Harry, H. (1998). *Making friends: The influences of culture and development*. Baltimore: Brookes.

Overton, S., & Rausch, J. L. (2002). Peer relationships as support for children with disabilities: An analysis of mothers' goals and indicators for friendship. *Focus on Autism and Other Developmental Disabilities, 17*, 11–29.

Parke, R. D., Burks, V. M., Carson, J. L., Neville, B., & Boyum, L. A. (1994). Family-peer relationships: A tripartite model. In R. D. Parke & S. G. Kellam (Eds.), *Exploring family relationships with other social contexts* (pp. 115–145). Hillsdale, NJ: Lawrence Erlbaum Associates.

Richardson, P., & Schwartz, I. (1998). Making friends in preschool: Friendship patterns of young children with disabilities. In L. H. Meyer, H. Park, M. Grenot-Scheyer, I. S. Schwartz, & B. Harry (Eds.), *Making friends: The influences of culture and development* (pp. 65–80). Baltimore: Brookes.

Sandall, S., Hemmeter, M. L., Smith, B. J., & McLean, M. E. (2005). *DEC recommended practices: A comprehensive guide for practical application*. Longmont, CO: Sopris West.

Staub, D., Schwartz, I. S., Gallucci, C., & Peck, C. A. (1994). Four portraits of friendships at an inclusive school. *Journal of the Association for Persons With Severe Handicaps, 19*, 314–325.

Strully, J., & Strully, C. (1996). Friendships as an educational goal: What we have learned and where we are headed. In S. Stainback & W. Stainback (Eds.), *Inclusion: A guide for educators* (pp.141–169). Baltimore: Brookes.

Taylor, A. S., Peterson, C. A., McMurray-Schwarz, P., & Guillou, T. S. (2002). Social skills interventions: Not just for children with special needs. *Young Exceptional Children, 5*, 19–26.

Turnbull, A. P., Pereira, L., & Blue-Banning, M. J. (1999). Parents' facilitation of friendships between their children with a disability and friends without a disability. *Journal of the Association for Persons With Severe Handicaps, 24*, 85–99.

Youngblade, L. M., & Belsky, J. (1992). Parent-child antecedents of 5-year-olds' close friendships: A longitudinal analysis. *Developmental Psychology, 28*, 700–713.

Authentic Assessment in the Inclusive Classroom: Using Portfolios to Document Change and Modify Curriculum

Ellen M. Lynch, Ed.D.,
The University of Cincinnati, OH

In today's educational climate of evidence-based practice, academic content standards, and federal accountability legislation, teachers of young children are expected to be competent in planning and implementing curriculum as well as in conducting and interpreting assessments (National Association for the Education of Young Children [NAEYC], 2001; National Council for Accreditation of Teacher Education/Council for Exceptional Children, 2002). Moreover, educators must possess the ability to adapt their curriculum based on the data received from the assessment process.

For some teachers, the term *assessment* may evoke the negative reactions that have come to be associated with implementing conventional, decontextualized testing practices. In truth, assessment should be viewed as the systematic collection of information about a child across settings and over time (Greenspan & Meisels, 1996; Neisworth & Bagnato, 2004). In addition, the assessment process should be flexible, conducted in the child's natural environment, and include observation, documentation, and input from families (NAEYC/National Association of Early Childhood Specialists in State Departments of Education [NAECSSDE], 2003; Neisworth & Bagnato, 2005).

The growing dissatisfaction with traditional assessment methods has led many educators to explore more contextualized and authentic strategies for examining a child's growth and development. Portfolio assessment has emerged as a valuable tool for teachers interested in collecting data that provides a comprehensive view of a child's abilities while at the same time meeting the guidelines for best practice as identified by the National Association for the Education of Young Children (NAEYC), the National Association of Early Childhood Specialists in State Departments of Education (NAECSSDE; NAEYC/NAESSDE, 2003), and the Division for Early Childhood of the Council for Exceptional Children (Neisworth & Bagnato, 2005).

A portfolio is a tool that can be used to collect documentation of a child's growth and development over time. However, portfolio assessment is more than a compilation of unrelated writing samples, photographs, and drawings. As teachers implement this approach to assessment, they systematically observe and document children's behavior and activities, collect work samples, reflect on the significance of what has been observed, and complete the assessment cycle by using the data for curricular adaptation and/or demonstrating achievement of specified goals (MacDonald, 1997; Nilsen, 2004).

The purpose of this article is to provide guidelines for preparing and implementing portfolio assessment in the inclusive classroom including strategies for using data for curriculum planning and change. The information presented here is anchored in the belief that portfolio development is an ongoing, individualized assessment process, grounded in child and family interests and priorities, which documents a child's progress in a naturalistic environment where children learn best. The discussion begins with a brief presentation of the benefits of portfolio assessment, followed by a detailed description of the process of developing and implementing a portfolio assessment, and closes with a look at completing the portfolio assessment cycle through analysis, planning, and modification.

Benefits of Portfolio Assessment

Portfolio assessment is particularly valuable for teachers wishing to obtain comprehensive information about a child's developmental progress and to collect data to inform the instructional planning process. The following six benefits of using a portfolio assessment process have been identified: (1) data collected in natural settings, (2) integration of assessment and curriculum, (3) multifaceted areas and input, (4) organized information, (5) active child participation, and (6) inclusion of diverse learners. Let's look at each in turn briefly.

Data Collected in Natural Settings

Teacher observation is conducted and work samples are collected while children are engaged in typical routines and activities in the familiar classroom setting. This is significant in that it is in such situations and environments that children are more likely to demonstrate their true abilities (Gronlund & Engle, 2001; Hills, 1993; Neisworth & Bagnato, 2004). Moreover, as data are collected over time, even small changes in children's abilities and functional behavior are noted (Losardo & Notari-Syverson, 2001).

Integration of Assessment and Curriculum

The portfolio assessment process is completely integrated within the classroom curriculum. As teacher observations, work samples, and other documentation are added to the portfolio, an individual child's progress can be examined readily, and curricular adaptations can be made quickly. The accuracy and richness of the portfolio assessment data provide a meaningful basis on which to revise curriculum, instructional practices, and individualized education plans (IEPs; Lynch & Struewing, 2002). Moreover, the portfolio process can provide evidence of children's progress toward meeting state curriculum standards (Helm & Gronlund, 2000).

Multifaceted Approach

An important indicator of an effective assessment plan is that it involves the collection of information about a child's development in all areas from multiple sources (NAEYC & NAECSSDE, 2003). This approach enables parents, teachers, and all professionals who work with the student to gain a picture of the whole child rather than focusing on narrow skill sets.

Families should be viewed as an integral part of the portfolio assessment process (Meisels & Atkins-Burnett, 2000; NAEYC & NAECSSDE, 2003; Neisworth & Bagnato, 2005). Parents, siblings, and others who spend time with a child can provide valuable information and interpretations about behaviors, interests, and challenges that may not be uncovered in the classroom. In addition to the classroom teacher, other adults who interact with children in the school setting should be included on the portfolio assessment team.

Families should be viewed as an integral part of the portfolio assessment process.

Certainly, this multifaceted approach is desirable for every child in the classroom. For parents and teachers of children with disabilities, however, there is an added benefit. Portfolio assessment may include documentation of activities and successes that are not part of the child's individualized family service plan or IEP, thus providing a broader representation of a child's abilities, interests, and needs (Lynch & Struewing, 2002).

Organize Information

Portfolios help teachers organize information. To be useful for assessing children's development and achievement, portfolios must be organized systematically. This arrangement enables the teacher to more easily determine where additional documentation might be needed. An added bonus is that portfolios, which are effectively arranged, provide a ready-made collection of materials, which can be used for parent-teacher conferences as well as for team meetings.

Active Child Participation

Children should be viewed as members of the portfolio team and therefore should be provided with opportunities to make decisions about what to include in the portfolio. Moreover, as children repeatedly review and revise their portfolios, they can be encouraged to reflect on their activities and the progress they have made over time. These experiences promote the development of autonomy, self-confidence, and positive self esteem (Losardo & Notari-Syverson, 2001; Shores & Grace, 1998; A. F. Smith, 2000).

Inclusion of Diverse Learners

It has long been recognized that standardized assessments may be limited in their sensitivity to cultural and linguistic differences (Neisworth & Bagnato, 2004). The portfolio process, however, can be used to collect assessment data for all children. Although the primary reason for using portfolio assessment may be to conduct authentic assessment, an important outcome of the process is that each child can come to be viewed as an integral member of the classroom community. Portfolios can be used as tools to promote inclusion of children with diverse abilities, needs, and backgrounds in that each child's portfolio is unique and reflects individual interests, skills, and capabilities. Moreover, children with language differences or limitations are able to share information about themselves through photographs and work samples (Morrison, 1999; J. Smith, Brewer, & Heffner, 2003).

Portfolios can be used as tools to promote inclusion of children with diverse abilities, needs, and backgrounds in that each child's portfolio is unique and reflects individual interests, skills, and capabilities.

Figure 1
The Portfolio Assessment Process

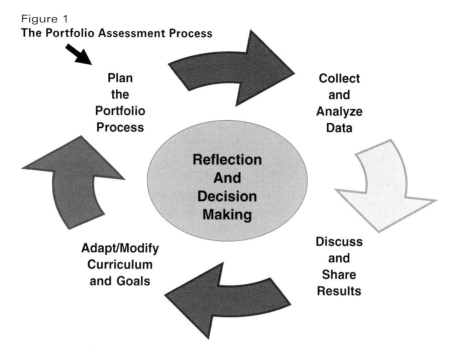

Plan
the
Portfolio
Process

Collect
and
Analyze
Data

**Reflection
And
Decision
Making**

Adapt/Modify
Curriculum
and Goals

Discuss
and
Share
Results

Developing a Portfolio System

As the teacher and other members of the education team begin the process of moving to a portfolio system, a clear understanding and support of the assessment, curriculum, and progress-monitoring process must be developed. Figure 1 provides a graphic representation of the continuous assessment process with each of the four critical steps: plan the portfolio, collect and analyze the data, discuss and share, and adapt and modify the curriculum. At the heart of the figure, and of course, the assessment/ curriculum process, is reflection and decision making engaged in by all members of the team. To accomplish the first step, planning the portfolio process, the educational team must engage in some initial preparation and decision making in terms of the process and then address setting up the mechanics of the system, or the nuts and bolts. Let's now look at each of these activities more closely.

Preparing for Portfolio Assessment

Prior to implementing portfolio assessment in the classroom, the educational team must engage in thoughtful reflection. Those who take the time to answer the following questions related to the assessment process will maximize the potential for successful data collection.

What Is It That I Wish to Assess and Why? As noted previously, all too often, assessment is conducted without attention being given to

■■■■■■■■■■■■■■■■

Without identifying what you will examine and why, you may have nothing more than a collection of artifacts that are difficult to interpret and that may provide little information about the child.

the what and why of the process. You must decide what it is that you actually wish to assess and your reasons for doing so. Will you examine progress in the cognitive, physical, language, and/or social-emotional domains of development? Are you intending to collect assessment data about specific content areas such as literacy, math, art, and dramatic expression? Do you expect to document progress toward meeting IEP goals? Without identifying what you will examine and why, you may have nothing more than a collection of artifacts that are difficult to interpret and that may provide little information about the child.

What Type of Portfolio Will I Use? After deciding what it is that you wish to assess, you must select a portfolio system to help you reach your intended goals. Numerous types of portfolios have been identified including the display, showcase, working, and evaluative portfolios (Gronlund & Engel, 2001). A display portfolio is similar to a scrapbook, which contains photographs of children engaged in various activities. This portfolio demonstrates the types of experiences that are typical in a particular classroom and can be shared with parents, administrators, and visitors to the classroom but is not used to assess children's progress. The showcase portfolio includes a child's best or favorite work as identified by both the teacher and student but is not used to inform the instructional process. It is the working and evaluative portfolios, however, that provide the basis for formative and summative assessment (Wortham, Barbour, & Desjean-Perrotta, 1998).

The purpose of the working portfolio is to provide a mechanism by which teachers can document a child's growth and development on a day-to-day, week-to-week, or month-to-month basis. The contents of the working portfolio typically include children's work samples; however, these are not to be considered representative of a child's best work but are to be viewed as illustrative of typical, everyday performance (Meisels, Dichtelmiller, Jablon, Dorfman, & Marsden, 1997). In addition, the working portfolio can include teacher observations, parent comments, a child's plans for future work, videotapes, photographs, and other items that are decided on by both the teacher and child.

According to Black and William (1998), the formative assessment process refers to "those activities undertaken by teachers and by their students [that] provide information to be used as feedback to modify the teaching and learning activities in which they are engaged" (p. 7). The development of a working portfolio is a type of activity that can provide the basis for formative assessment. However, it is important to recognize that the mere placement of materials into a portfolio does not constitute either formative or portfolio assessment. It is only as the assessment team repeatedly reviews and reflects on the contents of the portfolio, and as modifications to teaching strategies and/or curriculum are made, that true assessment occurs (Atkin, Black, & Coffey, 2001; Gronlund, 1998).

It is only as the assessment team repeatedly reviews and reflects on the contents of the portfolio, and as modifications to teaching strategies and/or curriculum are made, that true assessment occurs.

The evaluative portfolio enables teachers, school administrators, and parents to assess the degree to which a child has reached or met established goals, objectives, and/or curriculum standards. The contents of this type of portfolio might include a child's work samples, which demonstrate achievement of a specific goal or standard; reading logs; results from standardized and classroom testing; checklists; rating scales; and teacher and parent comments.

Although the purpose of formative assessment is to improve teaching and learning, the focus of summative assessment is on what a child has achieved as well as on the quality of what has been learned at the end of a set of activities or lessons (Bransford, Brown, & Cocking, 2000). It should be noted, however, that the line between formative and summative assessment is not always clear. Formative assessment data can inform the summative assessment process and vice versa. For example, a kindergarten teacher may collect writing samples throughout the year to document a child's development of writing conventions such as spelling, handwriting, and punctuation. These data could be used to make immediate decisions about how to modify teaching strategies to better meet the child's needs (formative assessment). However, selected work samples collected throughout the year might also be placed in an evaluative portfolio to document that the child has met a specific IEP goal or curriculum standard or benchmark (summative assessment). Conversely, information from the analysis of standardized achievement tests can be used formatively to inform the process of instructional or curriculum change.

Can I Use Portfolios With Other Forms of Assessment in My Classroom? Most teachers use a variety of assessments in their classrooms, some of which are required by their school districts and/or state departments of education. Recall that assessment should lead you to a picture of the whole child: strengths, challenges, needs, and current levels of development. As you consider the adoption of portfolios as a means of assessment, reflect on how the portfolio process will contribute to your understanding of the children you teach.

How Will I Maintain Confidentiality? No matter the type of portfolio you choose to use, the confidentiality of children's materials must be addressed. Will the portfolios be available for all to view? If so, when deciding about what to include in the portfolio, you will need to make sure that sensitive materials, such as test results, are filed in another location. You will also want to consider if permission should be granted before others view a child's portfolio.

What Happens at the End of the School Year? Again, this depends on the type of portfolio assessment that is being used in your classroom. You can give the entire portfolio or part of the portfolio to the child and his or her parents at the end of the year. You can also duplicate some of the contents for your own records. If you have a child in your classroom for multiple years, you will undoubtedly want to retain some documentation that demonstrates the child's developmental progress and achievements throughout his entire time with you.

The Nuts and Bolts of Portfolio Assessment

After careful thought, you have decided to implement portfolio assessment but are unsure of where to begin. You can use the following to questions to guide you: What should I include and why? How will the data be organized to facilitate progress monitoring and efficient data collection?

What to Include in the Portfolio?

The portfolio contents should include artifacts, which provide evidence of a child's development and/or progress toward specific goals, objectives, and benchmarks. The following items should be viewed as suggestions and not as a definitive list.

Letter to the Parents. Develop a letter for families that describes the portfolio process that you will be implementing in the classroom, and be sure to identify the purpose, how it will be used, and the parent and child's role. This overview can be given to parents at the beginning of the year or when a new child enrolls in your program. However, you may also find it useful to include a copy in each child's portfolio during the first few months of school.

Information About the Family. Including family information in the portfolio provides numerous benefits. Parent input may provide you with information about the child's life beyond the classroom. What are family

Figure 2
Sample Parent Comment Form

Today's Date: _____

Dear _____,

I was looking at your portfolio today, and I wanted to share this idea with you!

_____

_____

_____

_____

_____

From,

members' names? What do they like to do together? What is important to the family? This information can be extremely important in making decisions about individual strengths, needs, and possible challenges. Moreover, parent contributions provide a mechanism by which you can begin to establish relationships with the child and his or her family. Recall that confidentiality remains an important concern. Sensitive information from families should not be made available for other children or families to view.

Comments From Parents. As mentioned previously, parents should be viewed as important members of the assessment team and should be encouraged to contribute to a child's portfolio. Figure 2 provides a sample comment form, which parents or other adults who work with the child can use to record their observations.

Child's Self-Evaluation. Children should not only be part of the portfolio development process but also be included in the assessment of their work (Losardo & Notari-Syverson, 2001). As children evaluate their portfolios, they have the opportunity to develop their critical thinking and analysis skills. Adults should facilitate this process, especially for younger children, by reviewing the portfolio contents with the child and recording their responses to questions such as, (1) What is your favorite/least favorite item in your portfolio and why? and (2) What does this picture/writing/dictation/audiotape show that you have learned?

Checklists and Anecdotal Records. These tools can be used to record information about a child's behaviors, interactions, and interests (MacDonald, 1997; Shores & Grace, 1998). For example, checklists can be used to record the areas of the classroom or the activities in which a child is engaged most or least often. A classroom use checklist, if completed regularly, can provide the teacher with information about individual interests and favorite activities. Conversely, if you find that a child is avoiding activities that involve considerable fine motor coordination (or behaviors representing other developmental domains), you may wish to explore this issue further to rule out delays in this area.

Anecdotal records are concise, factual notes, usually recorded by a teacher, describing a child's behavior. If recorded regularly, anecdotes can provide the teacher with invaluable information about a child's strengths, interests, and challenges. Figure 3 provides an example of a form developed specifically for use in the classroom. Although memo pads can be used to record anecdotes, providing a predesigned form enables recorders to complete anecdotes quickly and systematically even if they have had limited experience writing notes. You will also note that the form provides a mechanism by which teachers can note that a particular anecdote provides evidence of progress toward IEP goals. In the sample, Ben, without being asked, shares a shovel and pail with J.K. The teacher has made a notation that this brief event provides evidence of one of Ben's IEP goals

Figure 3
Sample Anecdotal Record

Name of Child: _Ben_	(Reverse side of the anecdotal form)
Date: _September 27, 2006_ M T W **H** F	Additional notes/comments about the event/context:

Art	Blocks	Books	Computer
Dramatic Play	Gross-Motor	Group Time	Lunch
Manipulatives	Math	Music	Nap
Outside	Puzzles	Science	Sensory Table
Snack	Special Activity	Writing Center	Other

Area: Cognitive   Gross/Fine Motor   Language
Social-Emotional   Goal

Ben was in the sandbox alone. JK came into the sandbox and sat directly across from him. Ben had both shovels and pails. The two looked at each other for ~5 seconds (no talking) then B gave shovel/pail to JK. JK smiled and began to dig in the sand.

Recorder's Initials: _JAH_

in the domain of social-emotional development. Certainly, this example of sharing may provide evidence of Ben's developing prosocial behavior.

Work Samples. Most teachers collect samples of work, which can include examples of writing, child dictation, collage, drawing, painting, and cutting. If it is impractical to include an item in the portfolio, such as a construction made from styrofoam and straws, then photographs can be included to represent the work.

Audiotape Recordings. Audiotapes can provide important information about a child's development. For example, recording a child's reading of a book can provide data about language and literacy skills. Recording a child as he or she plays a math game with a peer can provide information about social skills as well as his or her understanding of mathematical concepts. Tapes can be reviewed by the classroom teacher, parent, or child and may be analyzed by a speech-language therapist or special education teacher who is working with a particular student.

Videotape Recordings. Video recordings may enable parents, teachers, and other professionals to gain a more comprehensive picture of a child's development and skills. This is particularly the case when information about specific skills that are difficult to document is desired. For example, if an IEP goal has been established related to the level of appropriate interaction during group time, video recordings may provide clear documentation of a child's progress toward meeting this goal through repeated recordings of group meetings over time.

Photographs. Photographs can provide teachers and parents with invaluable information about a child's abilities and interests. For example, photographs can document a child's developing head control over time or may provide evidence of a student's ability to draw letters and numerals. Moreover, inclusion of photographs personalizes a child's portfolio while providing documentation of a child's interactions with various peers, activities, and materials. Photographs can also be used to document group activities such as field trips, special classroom visitors, or group projects. Teachers, parents, and children may also wish to record comments about the photographs for inclusion in the portfolio.

Photographs also provide invaluable documentation of experiences for children who cannot or choose not to generate products to take home or to include in the portfolio. For example, a child with severe physical disabilities may have difficulty drawing a picture or dictating a story about a class trip to the local fire station. However, photographs may be included in the student's portfolio to document the child's involvement in the experience. Equally important is the fact that parents have the opportunity to see their child as an active and included part of the classroom.

Journal Pages and Book Logs. Many teachers use journal writing and book logs in their classrooms to encourage the development of reading and writing. Children can be encouraged to include journal entries in their portfolios along with drawings they have completed that illustrate their writings. When needed, adaptations should be provided to enable all children the opportunity to engage in journaling. Photocopies of journal writing can also be included rather than the original work. Book logs, which provide a listing of books read by each child at school and/or home, are also appropriate additions to a portfolio.

Organizing and Storing Portfolios and Their Contents

The previous discussion presented the types of items that might be placed in a child's portfolio. It is now important to make a decision about how you will organize and store the portfolios as well as the information that is contained within them.

There are numerous items that can be used as repositories for the data and items you collect including three-ring binders, file folders of various types, printer paper boxes, and plastic storage containers. Your selection will be determined, in part, by cost, storage space concerns, whether you wish to reuse the container, and the types of items you will include in the portfolio. As you develop your portfolio system, you may find it helpful to consider the following suggestions.

Select a Storage Container. The goals that you have for conducting portfolio assessment will help to determine the individual sections of your storage container. For example, you might decide to arrange your portfolios by developmental domain: language, cognitive, social-emotional, and physical. You can also choose to divide the portfolios into sections representing IEP goals or various classroom areas and activities.

Locate Portfolios so That They Are Easily Accessible. Portfolios should be located in an area that provides easy access for all individuals who are permitted to review or to contribute to the portfolio. If you share a classroom or are concerned about confidentiality, you can place portfolios on a cart that can be wheeled into and out of the classroom. It is helpful to place materials near the portfolios that might be needed by contributors such as pencils, markers, lined and unlined paper, a hole punch, tape, glue sticks, mounting sheets for photographs (discussed below), and parent comment forms. You may also find it beneficial to place a box in this area to collect items that are to be added to the portfolios.

Develop a System to Organize Photographs. Because photographs can be such a valuable source of information and are easy to generate, you may find that you quickly amass a large collection. As a result, you will want to consider how you will manage your photos. Photographs that are to be included in portfolios can be attached to mounting pages that have been prepared in advance. These are typically 8½- × 11-inch sheets of paper with lines drawn across the bottom that can be used to record information or dictation from children about the photo.

Completing the Portfolio Assessment Cycle: Analysis, Planning, and Modification

The previous discussion focused on the process of how to collect and organize information that might be included in a child's portfolio. Although this discussion is extremely important, it is critical to understand that this is only the first step. After the data are collected, you must now turn your attention toward analyzing each child's portfolio to uncover patterns of behavior and developmental change. You must now answer the question, What does this portfolio tell me about the child? as well as determine how you will use these data to revise your curriculum and individual goals for students in your classroom.

As noted previously, a basic assumption of portfolio assessment is that it is accomplished through a team effort. Before the team meeting is held, a summary of the portfolio contents should be prepared and distributed to all team members. To maintain continuity and to support systematic record keeping, you may wish to develop a form that can be used to record information. Figure 4 presents an example of the type of form you might wish to generate for this purpose. The contents of your form should be consistent with the goals you have for conducting portfolio assessment and should be free of interpretation. That is, you should not attempt to interpret or analyze a child's behavior as you complete the summary form. Your goal is to record significant events/behaviors that have occurred since the last meeting and that will serve as the focus for discussion at the next team meeting.

Following the meeting, a team member should write a review highlighting the major discussion points. The review should be succinct yet comprehensive and free from professional jargon. Moreover, the report should document specific plans for modifications to curriculum and activities, identify changes to goals/objectives for individual children, and include an analysis of the child's current skills and abilities. For example, in Figure 4, we learn that Keisha was able to complete a 12-piece puzzle without assistance. During the next assessment period, it might be decided that puzzles with 14 or 16 pieces should be made available and that additional data should be collected as Keisha begins working on these more challenging puzzles. Figure 5 presents a sample form that

Figure 4
Sample Portfolio Assessment Meeting Summary Form
Portfolio Summary

Child's Name: Keisha Washington   **Date of Summary:** June 14, 2007

Prepared by/Position: Joanna Alvarez, Classroom Teacher

Domain/Area	Data Source
Cognitive Development: - Completed 12 – piece puzzle w/o assistance - Developed rules for new path game while playing with Jarrod and Maggie - Developed rules for math game played at home with mother - Played in the dramatic play area (grocery theme) every day for two weeks	• Assistant teacher anecdote • Teacher anecdote • Parent comment form • Checklist; Teacher anecdote; Speech/Language therapist anecdote
Language/Literacy: - Read *Brown Bear, Brown Bear* to Myah in the book corner - Dictated story about self, Katherine & Martine to accompany drawing then recorded in listening center - Wrote story about field trip to zoo including both invented and standard spellings	• Teacher anecdote • Speech/language therapist anecdote; audiotape • Teacher anecdote; Work sample
Social – Emotional Development: - Developed friendships with Katherine and Martine during past 4 weeks - Used problem-solving strategy to help settle dispute between Katherine and Martine - Established rules for play in dramatic play and outside with Katherine and Martine	• Teacher anecdote; photograph of dramatic play; drawing • Student teacher anecdote • Teacher, assistant teacher, student teacher anecdotes
Physical Development - Squints when looks across room - Walked entire balance beam several times without assistance in gym	• Teacher and assistant teacher anecdotes • Teacher and assistant teacher anecdotes

might be used for the meeting review. Note that space is provided for documenting the specific action steps and curricular changes that need to be implemented during the next assessment period.

Conclusion

This article has presented a discussion of the use of an authentic and contextualized approach to assessing children's development over time. Portfolio assessment requires systematic collection of materials and interpretation of data, which can be used to identify a child's current level of functioning as well as provide information related to curriculum planning and revision.

Figure 5
Sample Portfolio Assessment Team Meeting Review Form
Portfolio Assessment Team Meeting Review

Child's Name:_____ Date of Birth_____

Date of Team Meeting:_____ Location:_____

Team Members in Attendance: _____

_____

Review prepared by/Position: _____Next Team Meeting Date:_____

Analysis/Interpretation of Documentation	Action Steps/Curriculum Modifications
Cognitive Development:	
Language/Literacy:	
Social – Emotional Development:	
Physical Development	

Additional comments:

_____

_____

It is important to be aware that as teachers implement the portfolio process for the first time, there is the potential that their attention will be diverted from the assessment component of the process. Developing and implementing this system can be quite time-consuming, and it is easy to become focused on the products: the portfolio and its contents. However, it is crucial to remember that the ultimate goal should be to use the portfolio to document a child's development over time and to revise instructional, curriculum, and children's individual goals accordingly.

Note

You may contact Ellen Lynch by e-mail at ellen.lynch@uc.edu.

References

Atkin, J. M., Black, P. J., & Coffey, J. E. (Eds.). (2001). *Classroom assessment and the national science education standards.* Washington, DC: National Academy Press.

Black, P., & Wiliam, D. (1998). Assessment and classroom learning. *Assessment in Education, 5,* 7–74.

Bransford, J., Brown, A., & Cocking, R. (2000). *How people learn: Brain, mind, experience, and school.* Washington, DC: National Academy Press.

Greenspan, S. I., & Meisels, S. J. (1996). Toward a new vision for the developmental assessment of infants and young children. In S. Meisels & E. Fenichel (Eds.), *New visions for the developmental assessment of infants and young children* (pp. 11–26). Washington, DC: Zero to Three.

Gronlund, G. (1998). Portfolios as an assessment tool: Is collection of work enough? *Young Children,* 53(3), 4–10.

Gronlund, G., & Engel, B. (2001). *Focused portfolios: A complete assessment for the young child.* St. Paul, MN: Redleaf Press.

Helm, J. H., & Gronlund, G. (2000). Linking standards and engaged learning in the early years. *Early Childhood Research & Practice, 2*(1). Retrieved June 2, 2006, from http://ecrp.uiuc.edu/v2n1/helm.html

Hills, T.W. (1993). Assessment in context—Teachers and children at work. *Young Children, 48*(5), 20–28.

Losardo, A., & Notari-Syverson, A. (2001). *Alternative approaches to assessing young children.* Baltimore: Paul H. Brookes.

Lynch, E. M., & Struewing, N. (2002). Children in context: Portfolio assessment in the inclusive early childhood classroom. In M. Ostrosky & E. Horn (Eds.), *Assessment: Gathering meaningful information* (pp. 83–96). Longmont, CO: Sopris West.

MacDonald, S. (1997). *The portfolio and its use: A road map for assessment.* Little Rock, AR: Southern Early Childhood Association.

Meisels, S., & Atkins-Burnett, S. (2000). The elements of early childhood assessment. In J. Shonkoff & S. Meisels (Eds.), *Handbook of early childhood intervention* (pp. 231–257). New York: Cambridge University Press.

Meisels, S. J., Dichtelmiller, M., Jablon, J., Dorfman, A., & Marsden, D. (1997). *Work sampling in the classroom: A teacher's manual.* Ann Arbor, MI: Rebus.

Morrison, R. (1999). Picture this! Using portfolios to facilitate the inclusion of children in preschool settings. *Early Childhood Education Journal, 27*(1), 45–48.

National Association for the Education of Young Children. (2001). *NAEYC standards for early childhood professional preparation: Initial licensure programs.* Retrieved June 5, 2007, from http://www.naeyc.org/faculty/ college.asp

National Association for the Education of Young Children & National Association of Early Childhood Specialists in State Departments of Education. (2003). *Early childhood curriculum, assessment, and program evaluation: Building an effective, accountable system in programs for children birth through age eight.* Washington, DC: Author.

National Council for Accreditation of Teacher Education/Council for Exceptional Children. (2002). *NCATE/ CEC program standards: Programs for the preparation of special education teachers.* Retrieved June 5, 2007, from http://www.ncate.org/public/programStandards.asp?ch=4

Neisworth, J., & Bagnato, S. (2004). The mismeasure of young children: The authentic assessment alternative. *Infants and Young Children, 17,* 198–212.

Neisworth, J., & Bagnato, S. (2005). DEC recommended practices: Assessment. In S. Sandall, M. L. Hemmeter, B. J. Smith, & M. E. McLean (Eds.), *DEC recommended practices: A comprehensive guide for practical application in early intervention/early childhood special education* (pp. 45–50). Longmont, CO: Sopris West.

Nilsen, B. A. (2004). *Week by week: Documenting the development of young children.* Clifton Park, NY: Thomson Delmar Learning.

Shores, E. F., & Grace, C. (1998). *The portfolio book: A step-by-step guide for teachers.* Beltsville, MD: Gryphon House.

Smith, A. F. (2000). Reflective portfolios: Preschool possibilities. *Childhood Education, 76,* 204–208.

Smith, J., Brewer, D. M., & Heffner, T. (2003). Using portfolio assessments with young children who are at risk for school failure. *Preventing School Failure, 48,* 38–40.

Wortham, S. C., Barbour, A., & Desjean-Perrotta, B. (1998). *Portfolio assessment: A handbook for preschool and elementary educators.* Olney, MD: Association for Childhood Education International.

Alternative Assessment: The Pathway to Individualized Instruction for Young Children

Dawn C. Botts, Ed.D.,
Appalachian State University, Boone, NC

Angela Losardo, Ph.D.,
Appalachian State University, Boone, NC

Angela Notari-Syverson, Ph.D.,
Washington Research Institute, Seattle, WA

Linda is an early childhood specialist who teaches in a preschool classroom in a relatively poor rural community. She has recently had a new student enroll in her class. Daniel is a 4-year-old child who has failed to pass a language and early literacy screening conducted in the preschool that he previously attended. Linda contacts the speech-language pathologist who serves the preschool classroom and Daniel's mother, Mrs. Horton, and arranges a conference to discuss Daniel's needs. During the conference, Mrs. Horton is adamant that Daniel does not have a problem with his language development. She states that Daniel talks incessantly at home and is able to make his needs, likes, and dislikes known to the family. However, Daniel's mother expresses concerns about Daniel's interest in books. She states that Daniel will not sit in her lap or next to her and be read to and that he does not appear to even know how to hold a book appropriately or look at the pictures. In fact, the only way Daniel appears to enjoy interacting with books is when he is throwing them. Daniel's mother states that she is very frustrated and worried by these behaviors and that she is afraid that Daniel will grow up unable to read, like his father and grandfather.

Linda is now faced with making curricular decisions concerning Daniel. She has a clear understanding of Daniel's mother's concerns and knows that Daniel may need many language and early literacy experiences for development to occur in these areas. However, Linda is unsure of Daniel's present language and literacy abilities. The screening results supplied by Daniel's mother reported that the test findings were probably not representative of Daniel's true abili-

ties because of the uncooperative behavior he exhibited during the screening. The report stated that Daniel did not separate easily from his mother, that he would not attempt assessment tasks, that he insisted on throwing test materials, and that he refused to engage in play with the examiner. Based on this information, Linda decides to collaborate with the speech-language pathologist who serves the classroom in developing a plan to determine Daniel's developmental abilities. Linda and the speech-language pathologist both feel that a variety of assessment procedures should be used to obtain a comprehensive picture of Daniel's language and early literacy skills. This decision is discussed with Mrs. Horton who agrees with this assessment approach.

Linda decides to collaborate with the speech-language pathologist who serves the classroom in developing a plan to determine Daniel's developmental abilities.

Early childhood professionals must make decisions daily about the instructional strategies and supports that will effectively foster the language and early literacy development of children in their classrooms. These decisions are often based on the information gained from assessment procedures conducted by numerous professionals. Because information gained from assessment impacts decisions made about children's learning, the assessment process must be comprehensive in nature and must result in a holistic picture of a young child's abilities. Consequently, early childhood professionals are challenged to use a variety of assessment tools and procedures appropriately so that information gained through the process will accurately portray children's true developmental abilities and their instructional needs. This article examines the use of traditional and alternative assessment practices when determining the abilities of children at risk for language and literacy difficulties, as well as the use of information gained from these assessment procedures in the development of individualized instruction in these areas.

Overview of the Assessment Process

Assessment is the process of gathering information on children's performance for the purpose of making decisions (McLean, Bailey, & Wolery, 2004). Information obtained through the assessment process aids childhood professionals in formulating decisions regarding (1) possible causes for a behavior, (2) intervention strategies, (3) instructional modifications, and (4) evaluation of learning (Appl, 2000; Notari-Syverson & Losardo,

Figure 1
Measurement Processes

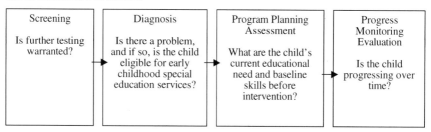

2004). Measurement can involve four processes with different purposes: screening, diagnosis, program planning assessment, and progress monitoring (Bricker, 1998; Losardo & Notari-Syverson, 2001). Figure 1 provides a schematic illustrating how these assessment processes are interrelated.

In the case of Daniel from our opening vignette, he has completed a screening, the first phase in the measurement process. Daniel's performance on the screening suggests that further testing is warranted. Therefore, the next phase in the assessment process is diagnosis to determine if he is eligible for special education services. Daniel will need to engage in a more in-depth comprehensive testing process in order to determine if there is a problem, and if so, if he will be eligible for special education services. The National Association for the Education of Young Children (NAEYC) and the National Association of Early Childhood Specialists in State Departments of Education (NAECS/SDE) (NAEYC & NAECS/SDE, 2003) as well as The Division of Early Childhood of the Council for Exceptional Children (DEC/CEC) (Neisworth & Bagnato, 2005) have identified key recommendations for assessment best practices. These include: (1) assessments should be authentic, based on observations of children engaged in actual tasks or during everyday activities; (2) assessment evidence should be used to understand and improve learning and instruction; (3) families should have the opportunity to participate actively in the assessment process; and (4) assessment should include multiple assessment methods, measures, and perspectives. Consistent with these recommendations, Linda, the speech-language pathologist, and Mrs. Horton decide to use both traditional and alternative assessment procedures.

the assessment process must be comprehensive in nature and must result in a holistic picture of a young child's abilities.

Traditional Assessment

Traditional approaches to the assessment of language and early literacy skills may involve the use of standardized, norm-referenced instruments and/or criterion-referenced instruments. Both of these types of instruments have specific characteristics and purposes and present certain limitations in practice.

Standardized, Norm-Referenced Instruments. In this type of instrument, the term "standardized" indicates that a set of behavioral guidelines or rules should be closely followed by the test administrator when using the tool. The term "norm-referenced" refers to the fact that a child's performance is compared to the performance of a normative group with similar demographic characteristics (e.g., age, gender). This comparison is used to determine if a child's performance can be considered appropriate for his or her age or if their performance is considered delayed. The results of norm-referenced tests are reported as standard scores, percentile rank scores, or developmental ages.

While norm-referenced tests provide information necessary for comparing young children's abilities, such as language and early literacy skills, to that of their peers, three serious limitations exist concerning the use of this type of assessment tool, especially with preschool age children (Losardo & Notari-Syverson, 2001). First, norm-referenced tests do not recognize the variability of young children's performance across people, contexts, and materials. Thus, assessment results may be questionable because the testing experience occurs in unfamiliar surroundings involving unfamiliar tasks and people.

Second, norm-referenced tests do not provide opportunities to observe children and families engaged in real-life tasks. Testing occurs in contrived situations that are not reflective of the everyday experiences of young children. Many norm-referenced test items are chosen for their capacity to discriminate between groups of children of different ages rather than for their educational relevance.

Third, norm-referenced tests do not provide early childhood professionals with information on young children's learning potential, nor do they provide guidance in making decisions regarding intervention strategies and instructional modifications. Because norm-referenced tests are administered on a one-time basis and standardization procedures require a highly structured testing situation, examiners generally are not given the opportunity to make modifications in testing procedures or to measure changes in a child's performance following teaching or assistance.

Criterion-Referenced Instruments. The second type of instrument, criterion-referenced, refers to an instrument that measures a child's performance as it relates to a set of standards or to a specified level of accuracy and stated criteria for a certain content area (Bagnato & Neisworth, 1991; Taylor, 2000). Criterion-referenced tests do not usually assess neuropsychological abilities such as word finding and working memory (Wiig, 2000). Items on criterion-referenced test are usually sequentially arranged within developmental domains or subject areas. Numerical scores are used to represent the proportion of knowledge the child has mastered and adaptations are allowed and encouraged to elicit a representative sample of children's behavior in optimal conditions (Losardo & Notari-Syverson, 2001; Wiig, 2000). The results of criterion-referenced tests can be used by early childhood professionals for curriculum planning (Losardo & Notari-Syverson, 2001; Sodoro, Allinder, & Rankin-Erickson, 2002).

While criterion-referenced instruments are better suited to provide information on how to individualize instruction, they too have limitations. Many criterion-referenced tools contain isolated items from various norm-referenced instruments, which invalidate using standard scores for individual items and limit educational relevance (Johnson, 1982). Additionally, the task of creating criterion-referenced tests to assess specific content may be a tedious process for teachers and other professionals to pursue. Other disadvantages of criterion-referenced instruments include their lack of standardization procedures and lack of information regarding reliability and validity (Sodoro, Allinder, & Rankin-Erickson, 2002).

Practical Limitations of Traditional Assessments. Returning to the opening vignette, the speech-language pathologist decides to administer a receptive one-word vocabulary test, a general language functioning test, an early literacy test that assesses phonological processing skills, and an articulation test in order to assess Daniel's language and literacy skills. All the tools in this part of the assessment are standardized, norm-referenced tests. On the day of the scheduled assessment, Daniel and his mother arrive at the preschool on time. Daniel separates easily from his mother and accompanies the speech-language pathologist to the testing area. Daniel readily takes a seat at the table and begins playing with some toys and interacting with the speech-language pathologist. However, Daniel quickly tires of sitting at the table and attending to test activities. He throws test materials from time to time and repeatedly tells the examiner that he wants to play "what me want to play." The speech-language pathologist cannot complete the testing she had planned because of Daniel's lack of interest in the test tasks. The next day, the speech-language pathologist attempts to complete her battery of language and literacy tests. Once again, Daniel attends to test tasks for a brief time and then refuses to continue test activities.

At the conclusion of the assessment, the speech-language pathologist has completed a portion of the planned diagnostic battery but does not feel that she has obtained data that is reflective of Daniel's present level of functioning. She bases this conclusion on several factors. First, she feels that Daniel's limited test-taking experience affected his response to many of the test items. More specifically, the fact that he was expected to interact with unfamiliar assessment materials and that he was expected to perform tasks (e.g., pointing to pictures, following complex directions, and recognizing whether two words rhyme) in a contrived situation had resulted in poor performance. Second, she feels that Daniel was expected to behave in ways that were not familiar to him. For instance, he was expected to sit at a table for extended periods of time, exhibit compliant behavior, and carry out directives given by someone with whom he had limited interaction. These conditions resulted in an inaccurate portrayal of his abilities. Third, she feels that Daniel did not have the opportunity to demonstrate his language and literacy skills in familiar, real-life activities.

The speech-language pathologist also has reservations about the use of the information she had obtained from the assessment in curricular decisions. She feels that the diagnostic testing results did not provide Daniel's teacher with the type of information she needs to individualize his language and early literacy goals or to make decisions about instructional strategies or supports that would aid in his learning. With these concerns, the speech-language pathologist realizes that she must gather further information about Daniel though the use of alternative assessment procedures.

Alternative Approaches to Assessment

New and innovative alternative assessment approaches have been developed to address the limitations of using traditional assessment with young children. As depicted in Figure 2, alternative assessment models (Losardo & Notari-Syverson, 2001) fit into three major categories: embedded, authentic, and mediated approaches. Table 1 further elaborates on the key characteristics of each of the three major categories.

Embedded Models: Where to Assess

Embedded models of assessment refer to methods in which multiple opportunities for children to demonstrate skills across domains of development are embedded in the context of child-initiated, routine, and

Figure 2
Framework for Alternative Approaches to Assessment

Embedded Approaches: "Where" to Assess	Authentic Approaches: "When and What" to Assess	Mediated Approaches: "How" to Assess
Naturalistic/Play-Based Assessment	Performance/Portfolio Assessment	Dynamic/Curriculum-Based Language Assessment

Comprehensive Ecological Model

planned activities, thus addressing one of the limitations of traditional assessment. This type of assessment guides the early childhood professional in deciding "where" to conduct assessment. Naturalistic and play-based assessment is a specific example of an embedded approach.

Three steps are needed to successfully use naturalistic and play-based assessment to individualize instruction: (1) determine location, (2) select appropriate procedures, and (3) determine the appropriate role for each member of the assessment team. Naturalistic and play-based assessment occurs within the context of play and typical activities. Therefore, the planning and implementation of these activities is crucial to the success of the assessment process.

The first step in naturalistic and play-based assessment is determining the location and time of the assessment. In Daniel's case, assessment could occur at his home, child-care site, or preschool depending on the types of activities to be observed. Assessment planning may also involve more than one professional. Therefore, members of Daniel's assessment team would meet prior to the assessment to discuss his behaviors and language and early literacy skills.

The second step involves selection of appropriate assessment procedures. The interview process should be used to obtain relevant background information about Daniel and his family. The examiner, in collaboration with the family and other team members, should select assessment tools and procedures that will provide multiple perspectives on Daniel's language and early literacy abilities across home, preschool, and community environments. Additionally, assessment tools should be selected that allow information to be linked from the assessment process to the intervention course, and then to evaluation procedures.

In the final step of the naturalistic and play-based assessment process, the roles and responsibilities of the assessment team must be determined. Daniel's family or caregivers should be invited to act as full participants in the assessment process and be provided with options as to their roles.

Table 1
Characteristics of Alternative Models of Assessment

Model	Characteristics
Embedded	• Measures children's performance across multiple activities and settings
	• Assessment activities may be child-initiated, routine, or planned
	• Predetermined behaviors observed and recorded by familiar professionals and adults
	• Assessment results reported both quantitatively and qualitatively
	• Focuses on functional skills to improve a child's independence and social interactions
	• May be accomplished through use of observations, interviews, and checklists
Authentic	• Measures children's ability to apply their knowledge in real-life contexts
	• Assessment activities developed specifically for assessment or part of daily routines
	• Requires collaboration to develop, gather, document, and evaluate children's behaviors
	• Assessment results reported both quantitatively and qualitatively
	• Focuses on profiling abilities of children through completion of real-life tasks
	• May be accomplished through use of formal tests, observations, and interviews
Mediated	• Measures children's responsiveness to instruction through use of guided teaching
	• Assessment activities designed to determine children's learning potential
	• Requires collaboration of team to determine how children problem-solve and learn
	• Assessment results reported both quantitatively and qualitatively
	• Focuses on children's learning strategies and problem-solving abilities
	• May be accomplished through use of observations and direct tests

Daniel's preschool teacher, his mother, and the speech-language pathologist meet to discuss how to best obtain an accurate and comprehensive
picture of Daniel's true language and literacy abilities. They choose to
move forward in the assessment process by using naturalistic assessment.
The team selects a language and literacy tool in the form of a checklist
to supplement the information gained through parent interview. The
team determines that Daniel will be observed by the speech-language
pathologist at home and in the classroom over several different days. The
assessment activities will include observing Daniel engaged in activities
such as identifying objects, people, and actions as he looks at books,
repeating phrases from familiar songs or stories, and using a variety of
adult-form sentences. Thus, assessment results will more accurately portray Daniel's true level of functioning and give the team information about
his strengths, weaknesses, and areas for concern.

Authentic Models: When and What to Assess

Authentic models refer to assessment activities in which profiles of children's abilities are documented through completion of everyday tasks
(Lynch & Struewing, 2001); thus addressing the second limitation of traditional assessment by allowing early childhood professionals to observe
children and families when they are involved in real-life tasks. Authentic
models of assessment guide early childhood professionals in deciding
"when" to conduct assessment and "what" to observe. Performance
assessment is a specific example of authentic approaches to assessment.
Performance assessment is a broad term that refers to methods in which
children are given the opportunity to demonstrate and apply their knowledge (e.g., being able to tell a story, draw a picture of a pet, create a shop-
ping list before a grocery store visit). Tasks can be developed specifically
for the assessment or they can occur as part of daily routines.

Portfolio assessment is a type of performance assessment. In portfolio
assessment, a child's work is collected over time for the purpose of documenting his or her efforts, progress, and achievements (Arter & Spandel,
1991). For young children, portfolios can include artifacts such as art,
drawings, photographs of modeling clay creations, videotapes, checklists,
anecdotal notes of teacher observation, and notes of parent interviews.
The use of portfolios is an effective way for professionals and caregivers to
share information about children's abilities and progress in familiar and
culturally relevant environments as well as in the educational setting. The
collection of artifacts that comprise the portfolio may be stored in several
ways. The childhood professional can use ringed notebooks, file boxes,
accordion file holders, or computer disks. The portfolio should be well

organized and can be divided into sections that are relevant to children's abilities and needs. Portfolio sections might include IEP goals, types of documents (e.g., drawings, anecdotal notes, parent interview), developmental areas (e.g., communication, motor, social), curriculum areas (e.g. literacy, math), or contexts (e.g., classroom, home).

Key components of successful portfolio assessment implementation are for the early childhood professionals to understand when to assess a child, to determine the type of skills they wish to assess, and then to select the appropriate method of documentation. In Daniel's case, this would involve assessing him while he is engaged in real-life language activities, such as playing with children in his preschool classroom or authentic early literacy activities such as reading books with his mother, recognizing familiar letters on store signs, printing his name on a birthday card for his grandmother, or inventing new words for a favorite song. Daniel's team would need to determine the type of skills they wish to assess (e.g., book/print awareness, metalinguistic awareness, oral language) and the method of documentation appropriate for use by family and team members (e.g., anecdotal notes, checklist, videotapes, work samples). The interpretation of data can take a considerable amount of time. During scheduled meetings, Daniel's teacher, mother, and the speech-language pathologist will need to pay close attention to details, avoid jumping to conclusions, engage in problem-solving, and make decisions about future observations and data collection.

Daniel's team decides that they will start slowly with this assessment procedure. Daniel's mother and the preschool teacher both voice concerns about their ability to observe specific behaviors and then to accurately document what they have observed. The team chooses to conduct performance assessment and selects book awareness as the literacy skill they will assess. Specifically, they will observe and take anecdotal notes to describe Daniel's ability to hold a book, turn the pages, and make simple comments about pictures in the book. These skills will be observed both in the preschool classroom and in the home setting. The team agrees to meet weekly to discuss what they have observed, to interpret their findings, and to decide on further observations.

Mediated Models: How to Assess

Mediated models of assessment refer to methods of assessment in which children's responsiveness to instruction is observed through the use of guided teaching; thus responding to the third limitation of traditional assessment by providing early childhood professionals with information on young children's learning potential. These models guide the early childhood professional in deciding "how" to conduct assessment. Dynamic assessment and curriculum-based assessment are specific examples of mediated approaches. Dynamic assessment is a broad term that refers to assessment procedures that attempt to understand children's learning potential through the use of examiner assistance (Swanson, 1996). The response-to-treatment (RTI) model is a recent application of dynamic assessment where children are assessed on an ongoing basis to determine appropriate levels of instruction (Kadaverak & Justice, 2004).

Curriculum-based language assessment may be used to determine the type of support children need in order to be linguistically competent learners in the classroom (Nelson, 1994). This type of assessment aids the early childhood professional in identifying potential gaps that may exist between the linguistic demands of the classroom curriculum and children's linguistic ability. Children from culturally diverse backgrounds or who struggle with learning disabilities would specifically benefit from these approaches to assessment.

To implement dynamic and curriculum-based assessments, a team of professionals and caregivers must identify the areas of the curriculum that are the most problematic for a child. The team must examine the contextual and linguistic demands of the settings in which the child spends time along with the curricular goals and objectives that the child must attain. Most states, for example, have identified early learning and academic readiness standards that children are expected to meet before leaving preschool (Grisham-Brown, Hemmeter, & Pretti-Frontczak, 2005).

In Daniel's case, the team must pinpoint the language and early literacy skills that he will need to be successful in his preschool setting. Following the examination of contextual and linguistic demands and curricular goals and preschool standards, the team must determine Daniel's abilities both with and without mediation by an adult or more competent peer. Next, Daniel's team must determine if he possesses the language and early literacy skills that he will need to be a successful learner. Together, the team will need to decide what types of mediated assessment tools and approaches will provide accurate information about Daniel's current level of functioning. Scaffolding, or guided teaching, can be used to determine his abilities with and without teacher support. Then the team must decide who will assess Daniel and when the assessment will occur. Finally, the team must monitor changes in curricular requirements and developmental growth of Daniel's abilities. The team will need to meet periodically to discuss his progress and to make recommendation regarding future teaching and support.

Bringing It All Together

Daniel's team identifies two areas within the curriculum that are the most problematic for Daniel: vocabulary and following directions. The team discusses the fact that Daniel does not know the names of many of the toys he plays with or the names of many of the pictures found in the books that the class reads together. In addition, the classroom teacher expresses concern that Daniel does not seem to understand how to follow many of the directions she gives the children, such as instructing the children to sit in a circle or asking the children to select a puzzle they would like to work on. She quickly adds that she does not think that Daniel is exhibiting belligerent behavior when he does not follow directions. She explains that it appears that Daniel does not understand what he is expected to do. After a short discussion, the team comes to a decision that it is important to determine if Daniel can learn how to follow some of the simple, routine directions that are given in the classroom and in the home setting. They decide to focus their observations on how Daniel attempts to follow directions, if he attends to the teacher or his mother when they are giving directions, and how he responds to the teacher and his mother when they give him feedback about not following directions. The group schedules a meeting at the end of one week to interpret the results of their observations. At that time the group will discuss possible strategies for teaching Daniel to follow directions.

alternative assessment can serve as a guide for assessing young children with diverse developmental abilities and provide valuable information for individualizing instruction, monitoring children's progress, and adjusting instruction to meet children's needs.

Because Daniel's vocabulary skills are also an area that must be assessed, the team decides that the speech-language pathologist should focus her observations on how Daniel attempts to communicate in the classroom with his limited vocabulary and if he is responsive to support that she gives him during play situations. The speech-language pathologist will report her findings at the meeting in one week.

Conclusion

Early childhood professionals routinely make curricular decisions and adjust instruction based on regular observations of children's progress. The framework for alternative assessment can serve as a guide for assess-

Table 2

How Alternative Assessment Methods Provide a Direct Link to Intervention and Evaluation

Alternative Assessment	Primary Methods	Implications for Intervention	Progress Monitoring/ Evaluation
Embedded Models			
Activity-based assessment	• Checklists • Interview • Anecdotal notes • Counts/tallies • Event/time sampling	Assessment provides useful information for identifying instructional objectives.	Allow for frequent observations and data collection.
Play-based assessment	• Checklists • Interview • Anecdotal notes • Counts/tallies • Event/time sampling	Assessment provides functional information on children's typical behaviors in everyday routines.	Allow for frequent observations and data collection.
Authentic Models			
Performance assessment	• Anecdotal notes • Work samples • Photographs • Videotapes	Meaningful goals and objectives based on assessment of the child's authentic behaviors in familiar contexts.	Multiple forms of documentation are gathered together and can be easily reviewed on an ongoing basis.
Portfolio assessment	• Anecdotal notes • Work samples • Photographs • Videotapes	Provides a tool for families to observe their child's behaviors and prioritize goals and objectives for their child.	Families actively participate in assessing child's progress over time; provides information on how the child generalizes the skill across settings and people.
Mediated Models			
Dynamic assessment	• Checklists • Anecdotal notes • Work samples	Provides useful information for identifying instructional strategies and modifications.	Assessment provides information on variations over time in types and intensities of assistance a child needs to perform a task.

ing young children with diverse developmental abilities and provide valuable information for individualizing instruction, monitoring children's progress, and adjusting instruction to meet children's needs. Table 2 provides an overview of different alternative models and methods and how they are linked to intervention and the monitoring of children's progress.

In Daniel's case, once the team has completed their initial assessment and prioritized appropriate individualized language and early literacy goals and objectives for Daniel, they will also develop a plan for collecting and sharing data on Daniel's progress on a regular basis. Alternative assessment approaches are consistent with NAEYC and NAECS/SDE (2003) and DEC (Neisworth & Bagnato, 2005) recommendations for assessment best practices. They are ideal when working with young children because: (1) they can easily be integrated into and across everyday activities and contexts, (2) they utilize observations and interactions with children and families involved in actual tasks and activities, and (3) they measure changes in performance following mediation by an adult (Losardo & Notari-Syverson, 2001).

Note

You can reach Dawn C. Botts by e-mail at bottsdc@appstate.edu

References

Appl, D. J. (2000). Clarifying the preschool assessment process: Traditional practices and alternative approaches. *Early Childhood Education Journal, 27*(4), 219-225.

Arter, J. A. & Spandel, V. (1991). *Using portfolios of student work in instruction and assessment*. Portland, OR: Northwest Regional Education Laboratory.

Bagnato, S. J. & Neisworth, J. T. (1991). *Assessment of early intervention: Best practices for professionals*. New York: The Guilford Press.

Bricker, D. (1998). *An activity-based approach to early intervention* (2nd ed.). Baltimore: Brookes Publishing Co.

Grisham-Brown, J., Hemmeter, M. L., & Pretti-Frontczak, K. (2005). *Blended practices for teaching young children in inclusive settings*. Baltimore: Brookes Publishing Co.

Johnson, N. M. (1982). Assessment paradigms and atypical infants: An interventionist's perspective. In D. Bricker (Ed.), *Intervention with at-risk and handicapped infants: From research to application* (pp. 63-76). Baltimore: University Park Press.

Kadaverak, J. & Justice, L. (2004). Embedded-explicit emergent literacy intervention II: Goal selection and implementation in the early childhood classroom. *Language, Speech and Hearing Services in Schools, 35,* 212-228.

Losardo, A. & Notari-Syverson, A. (2001). *Alternative approaches to assessing young children*. Baltimore: Brookes Publishing Co.

Lynch, E. M. & Struewing, N. A. (2001). Children in context: Portfolio assessment in the inclusive early childhood classroom. *Young Exceptional Children, 8*(1), 2-10.

McLean, M., Bailey, D., & Wolery, M. (2004). *Assessing infants and preschoolers with special needs*. Upper Saddle River, NJ: Pearson Education.

National Association for the Education of Young Children (NAYEC) & National Association of Early Childhood Specialists in State Departments of Education (NAECS/SDE). (2003). Joint position statement. Early childhood curriculum, assessment, and program evaluation: Building an effective, accountable system in programs for children birth through age 8. Retrieved December 20, 2006, from http://www.naeyc.org/about/positions/cape.asp

Neisworth, J. T. & Bagnato, S. J. (2005). DEC recommended practices: Assessment. In S. Sandall, M. L. Hemmeter, B. J. Smith, & M. E. McLean (Eds.), *DEC recommended practices: A comprehensive guide for practical application in early intervention/early childhood special education* (pp. 45-69). Longmont, CO: Sopris West.

Nelson N.W. (1994). Curriculum-based language assessment and intervention across the grades. In E. Wallach & K. Butler (Eds.), *Language learning disabilities in school-age children and adolescents* (pp. 104-131). New York: Macmillan.

Notari-Syverson, A. & Losardo, A. (2004). What assessment means to early childhood educators. *Exchange*, 72-76.

Sodoro, J., Allinder, R. M., & Rankin-Erickson, J. L. (2002). Assessment of phonological awareness: Review of methods and tools. *Educational Psychology Review, 14*, 223-260.

Swanson, H. L. (1996). Classification and dynamic assessment of children with learning disabilities. *Focus on Exceptional Children, 28*(9), 1-20.

Taylor, R. L. (2000). *Assessment of exceptional students: Educational and psychological procedures* (5th ed.). Boston: Allyn and Bacon.

Wiig, E. H. (2000). Authentic and other assessments of language disabilities: When is fair fair? *Reading and Writing Quarterly, 16*, 170-210.

Improving Outcomes for Young Children by Assessing Intervention Integrity and Monitoring Progress: "Am I Doing it Right and Is it Working?"

Gayle J. Luze, Ph.D., and Carla A. Peterson, Ph.D.,
Iowa State University

Providing effective services to promote development of all children is the goal of programs serving young children; this is especially important for programs that include young children who have disabilities or are at risk. Ensuring effectiveness of programming for each individual child can be difficult, and many children will need individualized interventions to address their specific goals. It is essential that these interventions be planned and implemented well. In fact, the Division for Early Childhood (DEC) of the Council of Exceptional Children (CEC) recommends practices addressing this issue with the guideline stating that, "Recommended instructional strategies are used with sufficient fidelity, consistency, frequency, and intensity to ensure high levels of behavior occurring frequently" (Wolery, 2002, p. 37). This article describes assessment of intervention integrity and child progress monitoring components teachers can use to help ensure effectiveness of individual interventions.

Ms. Youngston, an experienced preschool teacher, makes a considerable effort to meet the individual needs of all the children in her classroom. She studies related issues and talks frequently with other teachers about how to improve her teaching. A few weeks after Alana is enrolled in her room, Ms. Youngston becomes worried about Alana's development as she seems to be struggling in a number of areas. Ms. Youngston meets with Alana's parents to discuss her concerns, and they all agree that Ms. Youngston should share her concerns with the school's Intervention Team to get ideas for classroom adaptations to assist Alana. To prepare for the meeting with the Intervention Team, Ms. Youngston gathers information about Alana's current level of performance at school and integrates these data with information shared by Alana's parents. She reports that Alana has difficulty maintaining her attention to task, learning new concepts as quickly as the other children, articulating words clearly, and using words to communicate effectively with others. At the team meeting, Ms. Youngston shares this information with the team members who brainstorm possible solutions. They agree on an intervention to help address each concern. The team develops plans for each intervention, and Ms. Youngston takes careful notes about what to do.

Ms. Youngston has been working very hard to implement the team's suggestions for several weeks and is very hopeful that her efforts will improve Alana's growth. However, as she reviews the forms the team completed to describe each intervention, she asks herself, "Am I doing the interventions the way we planned them at the Intervention Team meeting? How will I know if the interventions are working?"

If you were Ms. Youngston or a member of her Intervention Team, could you answer these questions? The team did not discuss how to make these determinations. Monitoring intervention integrity could help provide answers to these questions.

What Is Intervention Integrity?

Intervention integrity, the degree to which an intervention is implemented as originally designed (Gresham, 1989), must be considered when determining intervention effectiveness. The relationship between change in a child's performance and the intervention that was implemented cannot be established without knowing if the intervention was implemented as planned. Intervention integrity is also known as treatment integrity, treatment fidelity, or procedural reliability/fidelity/integrity. While the terms are often used interchangeably, procedural reliability is actually a broader term, referring to examining all relevant variables that might affect the outcome of intervention implementation (including variables that are changed or manipulated as well as those held constant; Billingsley, White, & Munson, 1980).

The relationship between change in a child's performance and the intervention that was implemented cannot be established without knowing if the intervention was implemented as planned.

Measuring and maintaining intervention integrity does not by itself ensure a successful outcome. But, it does provide interventionists with additional information that can be used to make any changes necessary to increase the likelihood of an intervention's success. When an intervention is not implemented as planned and the intervention is not successful in bringing about the desired level of child change, the interventionist lacks necessary information to decide if this intervention was not a good fit for the child and/or the problem, or if part of the intervention necessary for success simply was not implemented. Monitoring

Monitoring intervention integrity provides the missing piece of data allowing interventionists to determine when intervention changes are needed.

intervention integrity provides the missing piece of data allowing interventionists to determine when intervention changes are needed.

Interventions implemented with integrity have been found to be more effective (Gresham, Gansle, Noell, Cohen, & Rosenblum, 1993; Noell, Gresham, & Gansle, 2002; Peterson & McConnell, 1996). While this is not surprising, several important issues warrant consideration. It may be that when intervention integrity is monitored, child progress is also monitored more closely and intervention changes are made in a timely manner resulting in increased efficiency and effectiveness. Or, it may be that when intervention integrity is monitored, the feedback given to teachers helps them maintain integrity (Noell, Witt, Gilbertson, Ranier, & Freeland, 1997).

Occasionally, teachers will report that they do not care about what makes the difference in a child's level of skill or behavior, just that the

desired change occurs (i.e., the goal has been met). However, most teachers do care about being effective and using their time and other resources in the most efficient way possible. Determining which interventions meet these criteria requires examining intervention implementation. This includes examining if the intervention was implemented as planned, and if not, what changes were made and why. If a child is not progressing as planned, intervention implementation can be examined to determine if the plan was followed. If not, the original plan can be reinstituted; and if acceptable progress is made, change can be ascribed to the intervention. If acceptable progress is still not made, the intervention planning team might determine that a new intervention may be needed to help the child develop targeted skills.

Interventions implemented with integrity have been found to be more effective.

Returning to the vignette, we see that no one on the Intervention Team working for Alana collected information about how Ms. Youngston was implementing the planned interventions, thus, if Alana's behavior did change, they would still be uncertain how the change was related to Ms. Youngston's efforts. The team did recommend several intervention strategies supported by research showing intervention effectiveness when all components are included. However, if they did not communicate this clearly, Ms. Youngston may have altered the interventions, being unaware that her changes could reduce the overall effectiveness of the interventions and/or decrease their efficiency by increasing the length of time Alana may need to reach her goals.

What Are Advantages of Monitoring Intervention Integrity?

The first advantage of monitoring intervention integrity is that these efforts require a clearly developed plan, thus ensuring that everyone on the team agrees about the specifics of what will be involved in the intervention and who will be implementing each component. This should make the team aware of any teacher training required to implement interventions effectively. Another important advantage of monitoring intervention integrity is enhancing intervention effectiveness. The team will know if interventions are working by closely monitoring implementation and simultaneously measuring child progress toward stated goals. As a result, the team can make more timely and efficient decisions. A related benefit might be that when interventions are monitored for implementation integrity, this attention increases the frequency and regularity of implementation; both are important for effectiveness. Too often interventions are begun with good intentions, but unless implementation is monitored, it is easy to be less diligent in continuing to implement the intervention frequently enough to have an impact on the child's skills or behaviors.

Another advantage of monitoring intervention integrity is that the team is more likely to continue to work actively with the teacher through the entire implementation process. They are more likely to help monitor child progress and provide feedback and support to the teacher during implementation of the intervention. Research has shown that teachers or interventionists are more likely to maintain high levels of intervention integrity when they are given appropriate training and feedback about how they are doing (Noell et al., 1997; Sterling-Turner, Watson, Wildmon, Watkins, & Little, 2001). However, since most intervention planning teams do not routinely provide feedback or ongoing support to interventionists, the interventionists themselves may need to initiate this process. This was true for Ms. Youngston, from the vignette. She did not receive training in using the planned interventions, nor did she receive regular support or feedback from the Intervention Team to help her know if she was implementing the interventions correctly, or if her efforts were effective. If a member of the Intervention Team had been working with her to monitor intervention integrity and effectiveness, she would have had answers to her questions earlier, and she would have had someone to help her make decisions about any needed changes.

teachers or interventionists are more likely to maintain high levels of intervention integrity when they are given appropriate training and feedback about how they are doing

How Do I Monitor Intervention Integrity?

Problem-Solving Process

Monitoring intervention integrity starts at the very beginning of intervention planning. A structured problem-solving process, such as the one suggested by Deno (1995), will help the team organize intervention planning. This general problem-solving process involves defining the behavior or skill of concern, brainstorming possible interventions to teach the skill, implementing the chosen intervention, and evaluating its effectiveness. The team cycles through this process as many times as needed to develop an acceptable intervention. The steps involved in using a problem-solving approach for intervention development and monitoring of implementation integrity are described in Table 1.

The team begins the process by defining child behaviors to target for change. Targeted behaviors or skills are those considered to be keystone behaviors pivotal to continued child progress or development in order to focus team discussions on those skills essential for academic and social development (Barnett, Bauer, Ehrhardt, Lentz, & Stollar, 1996). The behavior targeted for change can be a developmental or academic skill, or a social behavior. First, the behavior is clearly and objectively defined so everyone understands the concern. Then, information about how the child is currently performing (baseline data) is collected. These data can be collected using unstructured or structured observations, gathering permanent products, or videotaping behaviors of concern (Barnett, Bell, & Carey, 1999). In the case of Alana, examples of the types of data the team would gather include how long she is able to maintain attention to different types of tasks, the number of words she uses to communicate, and how often other children/adults understand her speech.

Table 1
Steps in Monitoring and Maintaining Intervention Integrity

1. Intervention Team specifies an outcome goal for child change based on baseline data about current skill level and desired level of performance.
2. Team agrees on an intervention to address goal. Intervention should be one with proven effectiveness.
3. Team clearly defines intervention procedural components (via task analysis, if-then decision rules, scripts, etc.) and specifies who will implement each component at what times.
4. Team determines how to measure intervention effectiveness *and* monitor child progress.
5. Team agrees how to monitor and maintain intervention integrity: a. Determines who will monitor the intervention. b. Decides how and how often intervention integrity will be monitored and evaluated for effectiveness and need for change. c. Determines type and level of support given to teacher/interventionist.
6. Team establishes a decision-making process: a. Role of team and/or individual team members in providing support for intervention implementation and monitoring. b. Number and frequency of future meetings to evaluate effectiveness.
7. Teacher and Intervention Team member assigned to provide support to teacher monitor and ensure intervention integrity.

After describing the behaviors to be targeted, the team then identi-fies a specific goal for child change and selects an intervention strategy. It is important that the team select intervention strategies that have been shown to be effective (Telzrow & Beebe, 2002). As the team brainstorms possible interventions, descriptions of the intervention can be couched in broad terms but once an intervention is selected, it is important that the intervention be planned very carefully. Each component is clearly defined so the teacher knows exactly what to do, what the child will do, and any decision rules that would apply.

Intervention components can be determined three ways. The first way is by using task analysis (breaking down a complex skill or task into smaller teachable skills). An example would be to identify each step that a child must do correctly in hand washing (Sulzer-Azaroff & Mayer, 1991). The second method is by using "if-then" decision rules, such as making a description of contingencies for each teacher and child behavior. For example, if Barrett follows directions to clean up, he earns ten minutes to play with his favorite trucks, and the teacher praises him and tells him how many minutes he has earned. But if Barrett does not follow clean-up instructions, he loses a chance to earn minutes playing with the trucks, and the teacher reminds him he will have a chance to earn time playing with the trucks the following day (Sulzer-Azaroff & Mayer, 1991).

The final way to determine intervention components is by using scripts. Scripts are guidelines for interventions that describe specific

actions to be taken either to prompt or to respond to the child's behavior and describe the teacher's verbal response in actual terms the teacher will use (Barnett, Bell, & Carey, 1999). An example of a script might be when a teacher gives a student, Caleb, a choice of where to work at center time by showing pictures of center choices and saying, "Caleb, do you want to work at the water table or art table first?" If Caleb makes a choice, the teacher says, for example, "You have decided to play at the water table, you can go there now." If he does not identify a choice, the teacher says, "Caleb, choose the water table or art table." Scripts are an effective way to develop intervention steps that are built on regular interactions or planned routines (Ehrhardt, Barnett, Lentz, Stollar, & Reifin, 1996).

Ms. Youngston realizes that she is often changing how she implements the interventions based on how well she thinks Alana did the day before. After learning about how to improve interventions by monitoring intervention integrity at a conference, Ms. Youngston goes back to the Intervention Team to clarify the intervention plans and outcome goals, and to develop a more systematic progress monitoring plan. Ms. Youngston and the Intervention Team review the interventions they had developed, define each behavior/skill targeted for intervention more specifically, decide to start with one intervention strategy to meet one concern, then decided which concern(s) to focus on next. They select using words to communicate effectively as the first concern for intervention. After gathering additional baseline data about how often Alana communicates using words, the team brainstorms possible intervention strategies. One team member with experience in this area, Mr. Moeller, refers to research articles about effective strategies. The team identifies a specific a goal for Alana in the area of communication: "When given a request for communication, and two or fewer prompts, Alana will respond verbally with at least a three-word sentence." The team outlines the specific intervention steps, basing them on empirically validated intervention strategies. For Alana's communication goal, they decide to use a combination of mand-model and time delay strategies (Barnett, Bell, & Carey, 1999; Wolery, 2001). It is at this point that the team first outlines specific intervention steps and decision-making rules (see Table 2). The team selects a new starting date and assigns Mr. Moeller to help provide training and support to Ms. Youngston as she implements this new strategy.

This level of specificity may initially be uncomfortable for some teachers, especially those working in typical early childhood classrooms or child care settings who are accustomed to a more child-directed approach. However, teachers often become more comfortable with the approach after learning how the techniques used for individual interventions can be embedded in typical classroom activities and routines, and see improved results for children who require greater support and structure to be successful in inclusive settings.

An important component of selecting an intervention during the problem-solving process is determining a teacher's preferences. An intervention has a much greater likelihood of being implemented as originally designed if the teacher views it as acceptable (Miltenberger, 1990; Reimers, Wacker, & Koeppl, 1987). This step is often overlooked, as many assume that teachers will naturally object to an intervention that they do not think will work, does not match the classroom, or is not understood completely. However, this is not always true. A teacher who is concerned with a child's progress may be willing to try to make an intervention "fit" in the setting, or the teacher may not be comfortable disagreeing with the group who suggested the intervention strategy. For example, an interven-

Table 2
Intervention Integrity Checklist for Alana's Communication Goal

Integrity Checklist for Alana's Communication Intervention	
Alana's Communication Goal: When given a request for communication, and two or fewer prompts, Alana will respond verbally with at least a three-word sentence.	
	Prior to working with Alana: determine when to implement time delay (activities and times of day) and how long the delay should be (number of seconds).
_____ 1.	Request communication from Alana (e.g., "Alana, do you want to play at the water table or the block area?"). If Alana communicates, stop. Respond to her communication attempts appropriately.
_____ 2.	Wait selected delay interval.
_____ 3.	Give additional prompt/mand if needed (e.g., "Alana use words to tell me where you want to play next.").
_____ 4.	Wait selected delay interval.
_____ 5.	If Alana communicates appropriately, praise use of verbal communication.
_____ 6.	If Alana does not communicate appropriately, provide model (e.g., "Alana, say, 'I want to play with blocks.'").
_____ 7.	If Alana communicates appropriately, praise use of verbal communication.
_____ 8.	*Child Progress Monitoring*: Three times per week, the number of prompts needed for Alana to communicate, and the length of sentences used by Alana to communicate.

tion may involve a teacher giving food as a tangible reinforcer, and the teacher might think this will disrupt the rest of the students and reduce the acceptance of the target child; however, the teacher does not want to disagree with the team if they think this is the best strategy. If the team does not ask the teacher about the acceptability of this intervention, they will not know of these concerns.

Important elements that contribute to an intervention's acceptability are ease of implementation, targeting development of positive behavioral or academic skills, and matching the intervention to the classroom context (Reimers et al., 1987; Schneider, Kerridge, & Katz, 1992; Telzrow & Beebe, 2002). A few minutes spent specifying the steps involved in the proposed plan and checking that the teacher understands and finds the intervention acceptable will help ensure the intervention's implementation and potential success.

Measuring Intervention Integrity

Once an intervention plan has been developed and each team member's role outlined, a system to evaluate intervention integrity is created. This is done even before the intervention has been tried with the child to ensure that the intervention will be implemented as planned. In addition, this step can serve as a final check that everyone understands exactly what is involved. One direct and practical way to measure intervention integrity is to make a list of the components or steps, including steps in a script or contingency "if-then" rules. The resulting checklist can be either very simple or complex depending on the child's needs and the complexity of the intervention.

Developing an intervention checklist appears to be easy, but many intervention teams do not include this step in their problem-solving routine and need practice describing each element clearly. Each component is defined and described in observable terms so that even someone unfamiliar with the intervention could understand the technique. Any steps that involve corrective action or are contingent on certain types of responses from the child also must be described, and it is helpful to develop ideas about how to handle a variety of scenarios.

To evaluate implementation integrity, a criterion for acceptable level of implementation is established. This is different for each intervention, depending on the component steps. One method of evaluating integrity is to calculate the percentage of steps completed correctly compared to the steps listed in the intervention plan. Another method is for the team to indicate one or more steps that are absolutely essential in the implementation of an intervention and to base integrity on the use of those steps.

A third way to evaluate implementation is to determine if the overall plan has been implemented correctly at least some identified percentage of the time (e.g., implemented the plan correctly 80% of the times it was used). There is no universal standard for the minimum level of intervention integrity to be maintained. This often must be determined by examining all the data related to intervention implementation and child progress. Very few studies report any level of intervention integrity, and even fewer report differential effectiveness of various levels of integrity (Noell et al., 2002).

After the checklist has been developed and the teacher begins implementing the intervention, the other intervention team members continue to work with the teacher to give feedback and guidance on intervention implementation, as well as on evaluating its effectiveness. The teacher uses the checklist as a self-monitoring tool while implementing the intervention. If the teacher finds that the checklist does not accurately reflect how the intervention is being implemented, then the teacher returns to the team to change the plan. Other intervention team members can also use the same checklist to monitor intervention integrity by observing the teacher during implementation. While interventionists typically have been found to monitor intervention implementation accurately (Luze, 1997), they often need help developing the checklist and working out implementation problems to maintain integrity. The intervention team continues to help the teacher by giving support and feedback. The schedule of this assistance should be established at the time the plan is developed, and future team meetings are scheduled to evaluate the plan as necessary.

Monitoring Child Progress

Another important tool to determine intervention effectiveness is frequent monitoring of the focus child's progress toward targeted skills. While most teachers are very familiar with a number of forms of assessment used in educational settings, they may not be as familiar with the use of frequent progress monitoring related to child outcomes. When child performance data are gathered and analyzed frequently, intervention changes can be made in a timely manner if the child is not making appropriate progress toward the established goal (Deno, 1997; Lentz, Allen, & Ehrhardt, 1996). To improve intervention effectiveness, these data are gathered, analyzed, and used for decision making by the interventionist on a frequent basis. Data should be collected while an intervention is being implemented or immediately after it has been completed (while it is best to gather data during implementation, it is not always feasible) so that the teacher is not simply guessing about how the intervention was implemented. The key is to analyze and use data to make decisions about the effectiveness of an intervention, not just to gather the data.

Ms. Youngston decides to use the intervention integrity checklist three times per week to determine if she is indeed following the plan and not making changes as a result of the previous day's experience. She knows that this intervention could be implemented at many times during the school day, so she decides to focus on morning group time, center choice time, and snack/lunch time. At first, Ms. Youngston carries a clipboard with all the intervention steps listed on it so she can refer to it as a guide, as well as keep data about implementation integrity. While she is interacting with Alana or immediately following an interaction, Ms. Youngston checks the steps that she implemented. She is then able to immediately review how well she implemented the intervention. She meets with Mr. Moeller weekly for support and feedback about how well she is implementing each step of the intervention, and how well Alana is progressing. Mr. Moeller uses the same checklist to monitor Ms. Youngston's implementation of the intervention, and discusses any help she needs to implement the intervention as planned, or help to plan any needed changes. Ms. Youngston is glad to have more information about how accurately she is implementing the intervention and more support in making decisions.

Mr. Moeller is not able to observe Ms. Youngston during class time, so they videotape her class during the identified integrity monitoring periods, and when he watches the tapes at a later time he uses the same checklist as Ms. Youngston to determine how well she is maintaining integrity. At first, Ms. Youngston maintained 100% integrity, but after several weeks it dropped to between 70% and 80%, indicating she was implementing the intervention correctly only 70-80% of the time. After discussing the intervention integrity checklists both completed, along with other notes each made, the teachers decide that Ms. Youngston is not waiting long enough for Alana to respond and is giving too many prompts for communication (not providing models). Together, the teachers decide on several private prompts/ reminders Ms. Youngston can give herself to increase her wait time and give models. Mr. Moeller and Ms. Youngston continue to meet, decreasing the frequency of meetings over time, discussing intervention integrity, as well as Alana's progress. The entire team meets after several months and are able to determine that Ms. Youngston has implemented the intervention as planned and that the intervention has been effective. Alana now communicates with teachers and peers independently. The results of this intervention and the monitoring done by Ms. Youngston and Mr. Moeller give the team valuable information to use in planning future interventions of this type for other children.

How Do I Make This Happen?

Currently, you may be implementing intervention plans without monitoring intervention integrity and may be wondering how you can get your team to begin this process. First, obtain support from your intervention planning team to include this new step. Then assign an intervention planning team member to each teacher implementing an intervention. This member's role is to provide feedback and support, as well as monitoring to ensure that intervention integrity exists. This person can be different for each teacher or intervention. The process may feel awkward initially, but with practice it will go more smoothly. This process may also sound like a lot of work. At first, it may seem that this time might be better spent working with children. However, it is best to ensure that the time spent interacting with children is maximally effective, rather than implementing interventions that seem like good ideas but may not change children's skills in desired ways. Monitoring intervention integrity is one tool that can be used to ensure that your efforts are both efficient and effective.

At the end of the school year, Ms. Youngston and the other Intervention Team members share information from the integrity checklists and the progress monitoring data with Alana's parents and the receiving kindergarten teachers. They find the information helpful in planning for the coming school year. The Intervention Team at Ms. Youngston's school had been wondering for some time how effective their team was when helping teachers plan interventions. After the team's success helping Ms. Youngston use intervention integrity checklists, they meet with their administrators and request additional training in operating effective problem-solving teams and integrating the use of intervention integrity checklists into their routine practice. They plan to use the process with all their intervention planning in the future.

Note

You can reach Gayle J. Luze by e-mail at gluze@iastate.edu

References

Barnett, D. W., Bauer, A. M., Ehrhardt, K. E., Lentz, F. E., & Stollar, S. A. (1996). Keystone targets for change: Planning for widespread positive consequences. *School Psychology Quarterly, 11,* 95-117.

Barnett, D. W., Bell, S. H., & Carey, K. T. (1999). *Designing preschool interventions: A practitioner's guide.* New York: Guilford.

Billingsley, F., White, O. R., & Munson, R. (1980). Procedural reliability: A rationale and an example. *Behavioral Assessment, 2,* 229-241.

Deno, S. L. (1995). School psychologist as problem solver. In A. Thomas & J. Grimes (Eds.), *Best practices in school psychology III* (pp. 471-484). Bethesda, MD: National Association of School Psychologists (NASP).

Deno, S. L. (1997). Whether thou goest . . . Perspectives on progress monitoring. In J. W. Lloyd, E. J. Kameenui, & D. Chard (Eds.), *Issues in educating students with disabilities* (pp. 77-99). Mahwah, NJ: Lawrence Erlbaum.

Ehrhardt, K. E., Barnett, D. W., Lentz, Jr., F. E., Stollar, S. A., & Reifin, L. H. (1996). Innovative methodology in ecological consultation: Use of scripts to promote treatment acceptability and integrity. *School Psychology Quarterly, 11*, 149-168.

Gresham, F. M. (1989). Assessment of treatment integrity in school consultation and prereferral intervention. *School Psychology Review, 18*, 37-50.

Gresham, F. M., Gansle, K. A., Noell, G. H., Cohen, S., & Rosenblum, S. (1993). Treatment integrity of school-based behavioral intervention studies: 1980-1990. *School Psychology Review, 22*, 254-272.

Lentz, Jr., F. E., Allen, S. J., & Ehrhardt, K. E. (1996). The conceptual elements of strong interventions in school settings. *School Psychology Quarterly, 11*, 118-136.

Luze, G. J. (1997). *The relationship of intervention acceptability and integrity in general classroom interventions*. Unpublished doctoral dissertation, Iowa State University, Ames.

Miltenberger, R. G. (1990). Assessment of treatment acceptability: A review of the literature. *Topics in Early Childhood Special Education, 10*, 24-38.

Noell, G. H., Gresham, F. M., & Gansle, K. A. (2002). Does treatment integrity matter? A preliminary investigation of instructional implementation and mathematics performance. *Journal of Behavioral Education, 11*, 51-67.

Noell, G. H., Witt, J. C., Gilbertson, D. N., Ranier, D. D., & Freeland, J. T. (1997). Increasing teacher intervention implementation in general education settings through consultation and performance feedback. *School Psychology Quarterly, 12*, 77-88.

Peterson, C. A., & McConnell, S. R. (1996). Factors related to intervention integrity and child outcome in social skills interventions. *Journal of Early Intervention, 20*, 146-164.

Reimers, T. M., Wacker, D. P., & Koeppl, G. (1987). Acceptability of behavioral interventions: A review of the literature. *School Psychology Review, 16*, 212-227.

Schneider, B. H., Kerridge, A., & Katz, J. (1992). Teacher acceptance of psychological interventions of varying theoretical orientation. *School Psychology International, 13*, 291-305.

Sterling-Turner, H. E., Watson, T. S., Wildmon, M., Watkins, C., & Little, E. (2001). Investigating the relationship between training type and treatment integrity. *School Psychology Quarterly, 16*, 56-67.

Sulzer-Azaroff, B., & Mayer, G. R. (1991). *Behavior analysis for lasting change*. Fort Worth, TX: Harcourt Brace College Publishers.

Telzrow, C. F., & Beebe, J. J. (2002). Best practices in facilitating intervention adherence and integrity. In A. Thomas & J. Grimes (Eds.), *Best practices in school psychology IV* (pp. 503-516). Bethesda, MD: National Association of School Psychologists (NASP).

Wolery, M. (2001). Embedding time delay procedures in classroom activities. In M. Ostrosky & S. Sandall (Eds.), *Young Exceptional Children Monograph Series No. 3, Teaching strategies: What to do to support young children's development* (pp. 81-90). Longmont, CO: Sopris West.

Wolery, M. (2002). Recommended practices in child-focused interventions. In S. Sandall, M. E. McLean, & B. J. Smith (Eds.), *DEC recommended practices in early intervention/early childhood special education* (pp. 29-37). Longmont, CO: Sopris West.

Evaluating Family-Based Practices: Parenting Experiences Scale

Carol M. Trivette, Ph. D
Orelena Hawks Puckett Institute
Morganton, NC

Carl J. Dunst, Ph. D
Orelena Hawks Puckett Institute
Asheville, NC

Comments from parents such as "It's nice to work with someone who understands how complicated MY life is," "I know when I make a decision about my child, my home visitor will respect it," "Now, I feel like I can help my child learn," and "I enjoy being with my child so much" are great to hear. These types of comments let early interventionists know they are using family-centered practices that result in supporting and enhancing parents' feelings of competence and confidence. Though comments like these are nice to hear, early intervention programs need to assess parents' perceptions systematically in order to determine whether such sentiments are occurring for all families in the program or for only a few

The Parenting Experiences Scale (Trivette & Dunst, 2003) described in this article allows program administrators and practitioners to quickly assess perceptions of parents' experiences regarding family-centered practices and parents' perceptions of their parenting competence, confidence, and enjoyment. Beyond describing this scale, this article provides information about why it is important to assess program practices and how a program might use this scale to gather information from families. Furthermore, it provides two vignettes about how program directors and staff could use the information gathered to improve program practices.

Program evaluation is an important activity in high quality early childhood programs (Harbin & Salisbury, 2000). However, deciding **what** to assess and **how** to assess it are questions that programs sometimes find difficult to answer. For a number of years we have been trying to help early intervention staff answer these kinds of questions by developing simple tools that obtain information that can be used to improve program practices.

Two of the concepts that are important for early intervention programs to assess are family-centered practices and parenting competence, and confidence. Both the Individuals with Disabilities Education Act (IDEA, 1997) and the Council for Exceptional Children, *Division for Early Childhood's (DEC) Recommended Practices* (Sandall, McLean, & Smith, 2000), specify that one outcome of early intervention is that parents of children receiving early intervention services should perceive themselves as capable of supporting their children's growth and development. Specifically, DEC's family-based recommended practices suggest a set of practices that, when used consistently with families, are likely to enhance the families' capacity to meet the needs of their infants and toddlers with disabilities (Trivette & Dunst, 2000).

Family-centered helpgiving practices are the tools staff use to build a relationship with families and to encourage parents to be active participants in supporting their child's development.

For a number of years, we have been developing various scales that measure the essential elements of family-centered helpgiving practices and three components of parenting: parenting competence, parenting confidence, and parenting enjoyment. Family-centered helpgiving practices are used to build a relationship with families and to encourage parents to be active participants in supporting their child's development. Parenting competence refers to parents' perceptions about their abilities to care for their child on a daily basis. Parenting confidence refers to parents' beliefs that they are capable of carrying out their parenting roles. Parenting enjoyment refers to parents' assessment of their affective closeness to the child. The *Parenting Experiences Scale* (Trivette & Dunst, 2003) brings together the results of our efforts to measure these constructs into one simple scale that can be used for the purpose of program evaluation.

Building on What We Know from Research

The influences that family-centered helpgiving practices have on parent and family functioning has been a focus of our research for some 20 years (Dunst & Trivette, 1996; Trivette & Dunst, 1998). Our more recent work has focused on the direct and indirect influences of family-centered practices on parenting abilities and functioning. The findings from two research syntheses demonstrate that family-centered helpgiving practices are associated with parents' beliefs about their abilities to obtain desired resources and supports for their children and families. For example, stronger beliefs by staff members about parents' abilities to get resources and supports were related to parents' positive judgments about their parenting competence and confidence, as well as parents' enjoyment in carrying out parenting responsibilities (Dunst, 1999; Trivette & Dunst, 2000). When staff used more family-centered helpgiving practices, such as helping parents get the resources they wanted for their children, parents were more confident in their ability to obtain resources in the future. These findings indicate that the ways in which early intervention practitioners (e.g., teachers, therapists, case managers, social workers) interact with families influence how parents see themselves as effective parents. The *Parenting Experiences Scale* (Trivette & Dunst, 2003) includes items that measure constructs which research shows are important practices and beliefs that relate to parents' judgments about their parenting abilities.

> *When staff used more family-centered helpgiving practices, such as helping parents get the resources they wanted for their children, parents were more confident in their ability to obtain resources in the future.*

The *Parenting Experiences* Scale

The *Parenting Experiences Scale* (Trivette & Dunst, 2003) is a one-page scale that assesses parents' perceptions in four areas, three of which relate to their experiences in early intervention programs, while one relates to their own parenting abilities. The full scale is shown in Figure 1. The first section of the scale asks about the amount of contact between the family and the early intervention staff. The second section asks parents their perceptions of how they are treated by staff from the early intervention program. The third section of the scale explores how parents feel in terms of their role as parents. The last section of the scale examines the extent to which families feel they can influence the resources and supports they receive from the program.

Contact with Intervention Staff

The first section of the *Parenting Experiences Scale* (Trivette & Dunst, 2003) contains two questions that ask parents about the amount of con-

Figure 1

Parenting Experiences Scale

Please circle how many times a staff member from your child's early intervention program has worked directly with your child during the past three months.							
Not At All	1-2 Times	3-4 Times	5-6 Times	7-8 Times	9-10 Times	11-12 Times	More Than 12 Times
Please circle how many times a staff member from your child's early intervention program has worked with you to help you promote your child's learning and development during the past three months.							
Not At All	1-2 Times	3-4 Times	5-6 Times	7-8 Times	9-10 Times	11-12 Times	More Than 12 Times

Thinking about all your contacts with your child's early intervention program staff, how often have the staff interacted with you in the following ways:	Never	Some of the Time	About Half the Time	Most of the Time	All the Time
Treated me with dignity and respect	1	2	3	4	5
Gave me information to make my own choices	1	2	3	4	5
Said nice things about how I parent my child	1	2	3	4	5
Responded to my concerns and desires	1	2	3	4	5
Respected my personal and cultural beliefs	1	2	3	4	5
Pointed out something my child or I did well	1	2	3	4	5
Helped me learn how to get resources for my child	1	2	3	4	5
Worked with me in a way that fit my schedule	1	2	3	4	5

Parents often have different feelings and thoughts about being a parent. Please indicate the extent to which each of the following statements is true for you.

How true is each of the following for you:	Not At All True	A Little True	Some-times True	Mostly True	Always True
I have fun with my child(ren)	1	2	3	4	5
I feel good about myself as a parent	1	2	3	4	5
I provide my child(ren) activities that help them learn	1	2	3	4	5
I enjoy doing things with my child(ren)	1	2	3	4	5
I feel I am doing the right things as a parent	1	2	3	4	5
I am the best parent I can be	1	2	3	4	5

Thinking about your involvement in your child's early intervention program, how much influence can you have in terms of getting information and supports you want from the early intervention program?										
No Influence At All					Influence About Half the Time					Influence All the Time
0	10	20	30	40	50	60	70	80	90	100

Source: Copyright © 2003 by Winterberry Press, Asheville, NC.

tact early intervention staff have with their child and family. The questions separate staff contacts with the child from staff contacts with the parent. Specifically, these questions focus on how many contacts the child has had with the staff in the past three months and how many contacts the parent has had with the staff in the past three months.

Family-Centered Helpgiving

The eight statements in the second section are family-centered helpgiving items that we have used in numerous research and evaluation studies (e.g., Dunst & Trivette, 2001a; Dunst & Trivette, 2001b). Our previous work demonstrates that effective family-centered practices include both relational and participatory components (Dunst & Trivette, 1996). The relational component includes practices that help build a relationship between staff members and families. The participatory component includes practices that provide families with opportunities to be active decision makers and which are individualized, flexible, and responsive to family concerns.

The participatory component includes practices that provide families with opportunities to be active decision makers and are individualized, flexible, and responsive to family concerns.

The *Parenting Experiences Scale* includes an equal number of items assessing the two components of family-centered practices. The four items on the scale from the relational component are:

- Treated me with dignity and respect;
- Respected my personal and cultural beliefs;
- Said nice things about how I parent my child;
- Pointed out something my child or I did well.

The four participatory items on the scale are:

- Gave me information to make my own choices;
- Helped me learn how to get resources for my child;
- Responded to my concerns and desires;
- Worked with me in a way that fit my schedule.

Parenting Ability

Our interest in parenting competence and confidence is derived from previous research demonstrating the impact of different parenting styles on child behavior and development (Dunst & Trivette, 1988), and how different professional styles of interaction strengthen or attenuate a sense of parenting competence (Dunst, Trivette, & Hamby, 2006, in press). After a review of the characteristics of parenting competence (Trivette & Dunst, 2002), we began to develop the *Everyday Parenting Scale* (Dunst & Masiello, 2003) to measure various components of parenting found in the research literature to be important to the development of young children.

The six parenting items included in the third section of the *Parenting Experiences Scale* (Trivette & Dunst, 2003) were selected from items on this longer scale. Both scales measure the following three components of parenting: parenting competence, parenting confidence, and parenting enjoyment. We have operationalized these three constructs in the following way:

- *Parenting competence* is defined as self-efficacy beliefs about one's capability to perform or accomplish daily parenting tasks and roles. The items were designed to capture parents' "beliefs in their abilities to fulfill different levels of task demands within the psychological domain of parenting" (Bandura, 1997);
- *Parenting confidence* reflects self-judgments about one's feelings concerning parenting roles and responsibilities. The confidence subscale assesses the parents' attributions regarding their parenting capabilities; and
- *Parenting enjoyment* is the self-assessment of one's affective relationship with one's child(ren). The enjoyment items are indicators of different aspects of parent and parent/child psychological closeness and attachment (Dunst & Masiello, 2003).

These three constructs are assessed on the *Parenting Experiences Scale* (Trivette & Dunst, 2003) using six items. The two parenting competence items are: 1. I provide my child(ren) activities that help him/her learn and 2. I am the best parent I can be. The two parenting confidence items are: 1. I feel good about myself as a parent and 2. I feel that I am doing the right things as a parent. The two parenting enjoyment items are: 1. I have fun with my child(ren) and 2. I enjoy doing things with my child(ren).

Parenting Efficacy

The last section of the scale has one item that assesses parents' sense of their own ability to access the resources they need from the program staff. This item measures what a person can do, not what a person will do, because the word *can* is a judgment of capability not an indicator of intention (Bandura, 2001). This self-efficacy item focuses on what influence parents think they can have in getting information advice, and support from the early intervention program that serves their children.

The *Parenting Experiences Scale* (Trivette & Dunst, 2003) includes less than 20 questions that reliably assesses a number of constructs important to early intervention programs. The development of the scale is only the first step of the evaluation process. Of equal importance is the completion of the scale by families so that the information it provides can be gathered from program participants. The following section provides information about how a program might go about gathering information, what might be done with the information once it is obtained, and how the information received might be used to improve program practices.

It is important to get the scale out to all families, encourage them to complete it, and provide an easy, confidential way for them to return it to the program.

How to Proceed

Program evaluation is often viewed as hard to do. Not to worry. It really is not hard once you have an appropriate scale. The next step is to decide how you are going to collect the information. It is important to get the scale out to all families, encourage them to complete it, and provide an easy, confidential way for them to return it to the program. Several programs have used the following steps when asking parents to provide feedback regarding their program practices and the outcomes of these practices.

- Identify families who have been in the program long enough to really assess their experiences with the program. For example, many programs that do weekly home visits choose to survey families who have been involved in the program at least three months after they were enrolled.

- Develop a cover letter explaining why the program is collecting this information, what will happen to the information, and how the families' confidentiality will be protected.
- Translate the letter and scale into the appropriate languages so that it can be read and understood by all families in the program.
- For each family, assemble a packet containing the cover letter, the scale, and a stamped, self-addressed envelope for returning the survey.
- Instruct staff to tell each family that a package will soon be mailed to them. Staff members should ask each family to complete the scale and return it to the program, stressing how important it is to receive a feedback from every family in the program.
- Distribute the packet to families during regularly scheduled visits and encourage parents to complete and return the scale.
- Staff who know that it might be difficult for a parent to read the scale should encourage the parent to ask a family member or friend to help them complete the survey. Staff should not complete the scale with the families.

Once the information is received by the program, the shortness of the scale makes it very quick and easy to enter into a data file for analysis. Though one can do rather sophisticated data analysis with the information from the scale, it is possible to generate very meaningful data to guide program improvement using less complicated statistics such as frequency distributions, *t*-tests, or correlations. Below are two examples of how programs have used information from the scale to make program improvements.

One example of how this information was helpful comes from a program that had both home-based and center-based services. When using the *Parenting Experience Scale* (Trivette & Dunst, 2003) as part of their evaluation, the program asked parents to indicate whether they received their services in the home or in the classroom setting. Upon inspection of the *t*-test results, staff found that there was a difference between those families who received home-based intervention and those families who received classroom-based intervention on their assessment of participatory helpgiving. The parents who received services in the home had higher participatory scores than those who received services in the classroom. This suggested that less participatory helpgiving occurred with families whose child received classroom-based services (Dunst & Trivette, 2005).

With this information, the program staff decided to focus on ways to increase opportunities for families who received services mainly in the classroom to be active participants in their child's experiences. Staff began to develop strategies to increase their ability to hear and respond to parents' concerns as well as strategies for increasing parents' opportunities to make choices for their children within the classroom setting. In order to increase parents' opportunities to influence what their children experienced in the classroom, families were asked to complete a very short form about what new or different things they had seen their children express interest in during the past week (cars, paints, new songs, etc.). From this information, teachers were able to ensure that these materials and activities available for the child in the classroom.

In another program, staff wanted to document the extent to which parents involved in their program felt confident in their parenting skills. The criteria for success was that 85% of the families completing the *Parenting Experiences Scale* (Trivette & Dunst, 2003) would report that they always *(i.e., Always True)* felt good about themselves as parents and felt they were the best parents they could be. When this program examined the distribution results from the scale at the end of the year, they found that only 75% of the parents reported that the two statements were always true for them. The 10% discrepancy between this result and their goal of 85% was considered by the staff as unacceptable.

The program staff then began to reflect on what they needed to change about their practices to increase parents' confidence in their own

parenting abilities. Two of the strategies they identified focused on the role staff played to encourage parents to provide their child new learning opportunities. One idea was simply to make sure that in every contact with every family staff would point out the things parents were doing well with their children. Another strategy was to help parents identify their own parenting strengths and determine whether they would be willing to share their expertise with other parents. Program staff decided the best way to do this was to ask each family about the areas of parenting they thought they were good at and encourage parents to share their strengths with others in both formal and informal ways. For example, one parent was asked to write a column in the newsletter about some of the strategies she used to successfully toilet train her daughter.

As seen in these two examples, this short, easy to administer scale provided information about how parents in their programs were experiencing family-centered practices and how families were feeling about their parenting abilities. With this information, staff was able to develop strategies for program improvement. The reader is referred to Dunst and Trivette (2005) for other ways of examining data from the scale.

Conclusion

Both IDEA (Sec. 631, 1997) and the *DEC Recommended Practices in Early Intervention/Early Childhood Special Education* (Sandall et al., 2000) make it clear that early intervention practices with families should be done in such a manner as to build the parents' capacity to feel confident and competent when parenting their child. What is needed is a means by which programs can evaluate the extent to which these family-centered practices and capacity-building outcomes are occurring with a majority of families being served by their programs. The *Parenting Experiences Scale* (Trivette & Dunst, 2003) offers programs a straightforward, one-page, tool built on well researched items with established relationships among the constructs to assess both family-centered practices and parenting abilities. With information gathered from families, staff will be able to develop strategies to improve their family-centered practices in order to enhance parents' sense of competence and confidence.

Note
You can reach Carol Trivette by email at trivette@puckett.org.

References
Bandura, A. (1997). *Self-efficacy: The exercise of control.* New York: Freeman.
Bandura, A. (2001). *Guide for constructing self-efficacy scales.* Unpublished manuscript, Stanford University.
Dunst, C. J. (1999). Placing parent education in conceptual and empirical context. *Topics in Early Childhood Special Education, 19,* 141-147.

Dunst, C. J., & Masiello, T. L. (2003). *Influences of professional helpgiving practices on parenting competence, confidence, and enjoyment.* Manuscript in preparation.

Dunst, C. J., & Trivette, C. M. (1988). Determinants of parent and child interactive behavior. In K. Marfo (Ed.), Parent-child interaction and developmental disabilities: Theory, research, and intervention (pp. 3-31). New York: Praeger.

Dunst, C. J., & Trivette, C. M. (1996). Empowerment, effective helpgiving practices and family-centered care. *Pediatric Nursing, 22,* 334-337, 343.

Dunst, C. J., & Trivette, C. M. (2001b). *Parenting supports and resources, helpgiving practices, and parenting competence.* Asheville, NC: Winterberry Press.

Dunst, C. J., & Trivette, C. M. (2005). Measuring and evaluating family support program quality (Winterberry Press Monograph Series). Asheville, NC: Winterberry Press.

Dunst, C. J., & Trivette, C. M. (2006). *Benefits associated with family resource center practices.* Asheville, NC: Winterberry Press.

Dunst, C. J., Trivette, C. M., & Hamby, D. W. (2006). Family support program quality and parent, family and child benefits. Asheville, NC: Winterberry Press.

Dunst, C. J., Trivette, C. M., & Hamby, D. W. (in press). Meta-analysis of family-centered helpgiving practices research. Mental Retardation and Developmental Disabilities Research Reviews.

Dunst, C. J., Trivette, C. M., & Jodry, W. (1996). Influences of social support on children with disabilities and their families. In M. Guralnick (Ed.), *The effectiveness of early intervention* (pp. 499-522). Baltimore: Brookes.

Harbin, G., & Salisbury, C. (2000). Policies, procedures, and systems change. In S. Sandall, M. E. McLean, & B. J. Smith (Eds.), *DEC recommended practices in early intervention/early childhood special education.* Longmont, CO: Sopris West.

Individuals with Disabilities Education Act (IDEA). (1997). 20 U.S.C. §1431(a)(4).

Sandall, S., McLean, M. E., & Smith, B. J. (Eds.). (2000). *DEC recommended practices in early intervention/early childhood special education.* Longmont, CO: Sopris West.

Trivette, C. M., & Dunst, C. J. (1998, December). *Family-centered helpgiving practices.* Paper presented at the 14th Annual Division for Early Childhood International Conference on Children with Special Needs, Chicago.

Trivette, C. M., & Dunst, C. J. (2000). Recommended practices in family-based practices. In S. Sandall, M. E. McLean, & B. J. Smith (Eds.), *DEC recommended practices in early intervention/early childhood special education (pp. 39-46).* Longmont, CO: Sopris West.

Trivette, C. M., & Dunst, C. J. (2002, December). *Parent ability scale: A tool for determining program effectiveness.* Presentation made at the 18th Annual Division for Early Childhood International Conference on Young Children with Special Needs and Their Families, San Diego, CA.

Trivette, C. M., & Dunst, C. J. (2003). *Parenting experiences scale.* Asheville, NC: Winterberry Press.

Resources
Within Reason

Supporting the Social Competence of Young Children

Camille Catlett, M.A.,
University of North Carolina at Chapel Hill

Here you'll find additional resources to support individuals and teams in connecting their ongoing efforts with national, state, and program accountability efforts. All resources listed are available for download at no cost.

Assessment and Accountability for Programs Serving Young Children With Disabilities

This article reviews issues related to the use of assessments in providing outcome data, discusses challenges in conducting valid assessments with young children for accountability purposes, and outlines decisions states must make related to assessment as they design and implement outcome measurement approaches. Considerations related to the use of standardized or curriculum-based measures are discussed, along with other choices related to the use of assessment for accountability.

http://www.fpg.unc.edu/~eco/pdfs/Assessment_Accoutability_6-27-07_.pdf

Child and Family Outcomes

The National Early Childhood Technical Assistance Center regularly updates this Web site, which includes federal requirements, planning resources, national organizations, state activities, and measurement tools related to child and family outcomes.

http://www.nectac.org/topics/quality/childfam.asp

Early Childhood Outcomes (ECO) Center

The ECO Center is a research project funded by the U.S. Department of Education's Office of Special Education Programs (OSEP) that seeks to

promote the development and implementation of child and family outcome measures for infants, toddlers, and preschoolers with disabilities.
These measures, all of which may be downloaded, can be used in local,
state, and national accountability systems. The ECO Center collaborates
with stakeholders and other groups concerned with outcomes measurement, researches issues related to outcome measures, and provides technical assistance to support states.

http://www.fpg.unc.edu/~eco/

Early Childhood Research Institute on Measuring Growth and Development (ECRI-MGD)

ECRI-MGD was funded to produce a comprehensive system for continuously measuring the skills and needs of individual children with disabilities from birth to 8 years of age. Their Technical Report No. 7, "Family
Outcomes in a Growth and Developmental Model," (http://education.
umn.edu/ceed/projects/ecri/ecrirpt7.pdf) includes family outcomes gen-
erated through a series of parent/family interviews.

http://education.umn.edu/ceed/projects/ecri/

Family and Child Outcomes for Early Intervention and Early Childhood Special Education

The outcomes were developed through a year-long consensus-building
process, coordinated by the federally funded ECO Center, that involved
input from and review by numerous stakeholders, including federal, state,
and local policy makers and administrators; local providers; family members of children with disabilities; and researchers.

http://www.fpg.unc.edu/~eco/pdfs/eco_outcomes_4-13-05.pdf

Family Outcomes of Early Intervention and Early Childhood Special Education: Issues and Considerations

Don Bailey and Mary Beth Bruder prepared this paper for the ECO Center
in 2005 to provide a review of information relevant to developing family
outcomes for Part C and Preschool Part B. It also contains a summary
of various frameworks that have been developed for family outcomes,
including examples of outcomes.

http://www.fpg.unc.edu/~eco/pdfs/Family_Outcomes_Issues_01-17-05.pdf

Implementing Results-Based Decision Making: Advice From the Field

Sara Watson prepared this document for the National Governor's
Association Center for Best Practices. She interviewed more than 50 lead-

ers in the field regarding advice on measuring the success of their supports for children and families by the results or outcomes they achieve for individuals, families, and communities. She covers various dimensions of results-based decision making, including strategic planning, which logically connects strategies to the outcomes.

http://www.nga.org/cda/files/1999WELFAREBARRIERS.pdf

The Power of Outcomes: Strategic Thinking to Improve Results for Our Children, Families, and Communities

In this essay, former secretary of human services for the state of Vermont, Cornelius Hogan, asserts that the lack of coordination between federal, state, and local government and programs has hindered the progress of our national education system, and he poses ways in which government agencies can work together to improve results for children and families. He writes that programs should employ an outcome and indicator approach that focuses on long-term responsibility and accountability rather than the traditional activity, productivity, and effectiveness model, and he discusses how by focusing on outcomes, programs can improve the well-being of children and families.

http://www.nga.org/Files/pdf/1999OUTCOMES.pdf

State Child Outcomes Activities

This ever-growing list of current state activities related to child outcomes measurement systems is maintained by the ECO Center. The chart of activities shows the assessment instrument(s) each state is using, when the child data will be collected, and the summary method to be used if using multiple sources.

http://www.fpg.unc.edu/~eco/whatstates.cfm#whatstates

State Preschool Accountability Research Collaborative (SPARC)

SPARC is a research project funded by OSEP to investigate appropriate practices for the inclusion of preschool children with and without disabilities in standards-based accountability systems. Practices will be identified from current research, perceptions from the early childhood community, and current practice in states. The project has developed state profiles on prekindergarten standards and accountability systems.

http://www.ihdi.uky.edu/Sparc/Default.htm

State Standards Database

Developed by the National Institute for Early Education Research, this database categorizes the language of state early childhood education standards and presents them in a common format. Data for 22 states; Washington, D.C.; and the federal Head Start program are presented. The standards database can be viewed by browsing either standards by state or standards by domain.

http://nieer.org/standards/